OFFICE ORGANIZATION AND MOTIVATION

OFFICE

ORGANIZATION

AND MOTIVATION

George R. Terry, Ph.D.

Consultant in Management
Chicago, Illinois

1966

Dow Jones-Irwin, Inc.

Homewood, Illinois

© Dow Jones-Irwin, Inc., 1966

First printing, July, 1966
Second printing, April, 1969

LIBRARY OF CONGRESS CATALOG NO. 66-24598
PRINTED IN THE UNITED STATES OF AMERICA

INTRODUCTION

THE managing and processing of office work have made great strides forward during the past several decades. This progress is viewed by many in terms of better office machines and equipment, improved analytical techniques, the efficient use of systems and procedures, and effective office planning. True, these are all vital; they have made significant contributions. But overshadowing all these gains and improvements is the ever-important and ultimate conditioner of all efforts, namely the effort of human beings.

Office Organization and Motivation deals with the people in the office, how they work together, how they meet work objectives, what motivates them, what scale of values they have, and what significant changes take place within themselves. The main theme is that people are the essential resource of the office; all office activities take place by, with, and for them. There are people in every office problem, there are people in every office effort, and there are people in every office success. Office management has improved and will continue to improve as the competency, dedication, and application of human knowledge and skills to office work are won, provide needed personal satisfactions, and meet the values deemed important by human beings.

In today's office management, the "happy family of employees" concept is as outmoded as the idea that a horse and buggy represent a modern means of transportation. Happiness cannot be directly given or gained, because it is not directly transferable. It is a by-product. What employees want is satisfaction from working with others who think and act about the work as they do, from accomplishing tasks that are well done, and from receiving just rewards and recognitions for their work achievements. It is this viewpoint that is taken in *Office Organization and Motivation*.

The material is presented in an orderly and logical manner, in nontechnical language, with the approaches clearly stated, and practical applications dispersed throughout the discussions. Anyone in, or interested in, office management at any level can benefit from reading this book. The material is applicable to work situations wherever people are involved, and this includes just about every type of office situation. The challenge of getting people to work together effectively and of motivating them to want to do their respective jobs enthusiastically is universal and basic in all enterprises, be they business, government, military, or hospital endeavors.

The accomplishing of office tasks is viewed as absolutely essential. Basic in these accomplishments are people inspired and enthusiastic about their work. An office employee's work life can be more satisfying and more meaningful when he is placed on the correct office job for him, is a member of a group with which he wants to work and be a part, and is gaining satisfactions from efforts expended and accomplishments won. This means that office organizing and office motivating are basic ingredients not only for effective management, but also for effective utilization of the human resource. That is, both the management member and the nonmanagement member profit from enlightened organizing and motivating. Human resources are viewed as being vital and basic. They should be handled with greater care than any other resource of an enterprise.

The very latest techniques of organizing and motivating are included in this book. Research in these areas has accelerated, many new ideas have been tried out, and a wealth of effective practices are now available to the astute manager who seeks and uses this fund of knowledge. Organizing and motivating are dynamic; treating them as being static gives rise to many unnecessary managerial difficulties. People change, and likewise our knowledge of their behavior, of how best to group their efforts, and of what means of motivation to use also change. The challenge is to recognize that these changes are normal and to use them to improve managerial organizing and motivating efforts.

Ten chapters comprise this book. Organizing is discussed first followed by motivating. Hence, Chapter 1 begins with considerations for the group and the formulation of an effective office team. Continuing with organizing, in Chapter 2, the discussion centers on establishing the proper work divisions and job assignments; and Chapter 3 takes up the attainment of correct organizational relationships, including, among other things, a discussion of authority, its proper use, the various types of authority, the degree of centralization, and formal and informal organization units. Next, in Chapter 4, office supervising is discussed, and the key position of the supervisor in both organizing and motivating is emphasized. Chapter 5 presents the fundamentals of employee motivation, relates examples of it, and includes some of the more common activities normally included in this general area. Following this, consideration for motivating office personnel by the major means of salary, development or training, and safety practices and trade unionism make up Chapters 6, 7, and 8. Chapter 9 points out that the human resource is very dynamic, why this is so, what opportunities this characteristic offers, and how a management member can take advantage of this persistency to change. Finally, in Chapter 10 is pointed out the assistance provided by an office manual in helping an employee to help himself and to guide his work efforts in the enterprise.

I have drawn from many sources in preparing this book. Practicing managers, various associations, clients, associates, employees, teachers, and friends have given generously of their assistance. The questions they posed, the positions they defended, the suggestions they made, and the agreements they voiced, have contributed immensely to this writing and they are all deeply appreciated.

Chicago
June, 1966   GEORGE R. TERRY

TABLE OF CONTENTS

CHAPTER ONE

THE BASIS FOR AN

EFFECTIVE OFFICE TEAM

Personal soundness is not an absence of problems
but a way of reacting to them.
—Donald W. MacKinnon

THERE is a great deal of truth in the oft-repeated statement, "The office is people." No matter how you look at it, in the ultimate, office work is accomplished by, with, and for people. That is, office management cannot be any better than its people. We sometimes lose sight of this fundamental truth with all the current spotlight and fanfare given computers, automatic office equipment and machines, new theories of office management, mathematical analyses, systems approaches, and office decor. It is not that these nonhuman and intangible elements of office management are unimportant; actually they are mighty important—sometimes vital and without peer. Their value, however, is what it is because of their relationships to man, his needs, and his ability to harness the tremendous capabilities and opportunities which are offered.

In our concern for human beings and the office we encounter basically two essential facets. First is the consideration of human beings as members of a group. The influence of the group upon its individual members is highly significant. What human beings try to accomplish and actually do accomplish are greatly conditioned by the group of which they are formally or informally a part. Second is the consideration of the human being as an individual—a special, sacred, and unique entity, capable of thought, innovation, development, value formulation, and tremendous production. Adequate attention to the individual—his capacities, his needs, and his satisfactions from the individual viewpoint—represent fundamental tenets in the employing, dealing with, and maintaining satisfactory use of the human resource.

1

Hence, in the study of office organizing and actuating, we need to consider men as groups and man as a group member, as well as man as an individual, in order to give adequate attention to this most important facility of any office—the human resource. For reasons of logic and simplicity, the group concept will be discussed first. This appears reasonable because management is normally thought of as dealing with a group and further, the constraints of the group normally affect each of its members or the individual's behavior. The group concept leads to the subject area of managerial organizing which deals with such basic questions as who of the group does what work, who reports to whom, what members are in which subgroups, and who decides what types of questions. Later in this book (Chapter 4) the individual concept is discussed. This stresses the efforts of managerial actuating or motivating. While this work applies to a group as well as to the individual, the more common approach is to consider actuating as being applied to the individual and includes emphasis on the individual's requirements for job satisfaction, means of motivation, personal development, and ability to cope with change. It is well to note that from the viewpoint of management organizing and actuating, the group and the individual concepts are closely interrelated—the group affects the individual and the individual affects the group. Stated more bluntly, managers must realize that organizing and its results greatly influence actuating efforts, and in turn, actuating activities affect the organization.

MANAGEMENT AND ORGANIZING

Organizing makes possible the effective operation of a group. It is the basis for an effective team made up of the various members of a common enterprise and helps blend together their efforts. Organizing guides the work by the various members not only to serve as a single coordinated force toward a common goal but also to utilize the particular individual specialty of each member toward achieving the major goal. In essence, the value of the individual's contribution is enhanced and, at the same time, the accomplishments of the group are increased. Every member, management and nonmanagement, knows how he and his work fit into the total picture, what he is to do, when and where he is to do it, and who, if anyone, helps him.

Organizing enables a manager to enlarge his scope of operation, that is, it makes it possible for a manager to accomplish much more than he could as an individual. It provides the means for using effectively the work of other people, and it sets the groundwork for the development of people. In fact, success in management requires effective organizing; failure to organize properly limits any manager's ability to manage.

Organizing provides a satisfactory climate for achieving an informed and satisfied work force. It avoids needless duplication of effort. It gets individuals to work effectively as members of a team, not separately as single individuals. It avoids confusion and misunderstanding as to who is to do what work. It prevents "buck-passing," an excessive number of managers and nonmanagers, and misinformed members of the group.

OBJECTIVE AND ORGANIZING

Organizing, like the other fundamental functions of management, is influenced and guided by the objective being sought. Organizing is, or should be, performed to achieve a definite objective, and this goal determines the organizational type and structural makeup needed.

To evaluate competently an office organization requires relating it to the particular objective for which the organization is designed. The question "For what objective is the group organized?" is a cardinal consideration in organizational efforts. The paper work required in one enterprise may differ from that in another enterprise. The centers for paper work processing are not identical in all organizations. Top managers' ideas of what paper work should be performed by what departments differ among enterprises. Some companies are local, others national, and still others international in scope. Also, some have only one line of related products, while others have multiple lines of products. These considerations help shape the objective and, in turn, are utilized to mold the organization.

MEANING OF ORGANIZING

Organizing is the allocating of the total work to be done among the work group, establishing the relative authority and responsibility of each individual who is placed in charge of each work component, and supplying the proper work environment. In organizing, a manager is concerned with (1) work—how to distribute it, (2) people—who is going to do what work, (3) relationships—what is the relative authority and responsibility among the "organization units" formed by the work distribution and the respective people doing it, and (4) work environment—what tools and workplaces will best contribute toward maximum work accomplishments. From the managerial viewpoint, organizing logically associates the numerous functions of an enterprise and the people performing these functions.

In addition, it establishes definite relationships among the people who are performing these functions.

Office organizing, like all organizing, is a dynamic, not a static, process. As a result, changes take place in an office organization; this is the common occurrence rather than the exception. Changes in an office organization take place for many reasons, such as changes in the objectives of the enterprise, changes in personnel, and changes in the conditions outside the office or of the entire enterprise. Organizing is an active, living entity—it is not a passive, rigid concept. The effective manager normally changes his organization from time to time in order to best meet the current requirements. Likewise, motivation practices are changed as more knowledge of employees and their individual behaviors is gained. The subject of dynamics in organizing and motivating is so important that an entire chapter in this book, Chapter 9, is devoted to it.

RELATION OF OFFICE TO ORGANIZATION OF ENTERPRISE

Since office work and its management are performed to supply a needed service to other major activities of an enterprise, it is advisable first to consider office organization in relation to the organization of the entire enterprise of which the office is an important part. It is common to think that in the typical organization, the major activities to be performed are production, sales, and finance. Each must be done satisfactorily if the enterprise is to survive. The creating of a utility for others is basic for most enterprises. This, in turn, necessitates selling efforts, so that the product or service is made available to buyers. The producing and selling efforts necessitate financing activities, in that ample capital must be obtained and maintained.

In addition to these three major activities, there are frequently personnel and the office, which are included to assist the main functions. Many feel that both personnel and the office are major activities, and that each should be accorded organization position and status on a par with production, sales, and finance. Sound arguments can be advanced to justify this viewpoint. In the case of the office, for example, the trend toward more and more automation, the use of computers, and the general recognition of the vital contributions of the office give increasing weight to this viewpoint. In keeping with this approach, many prefer the term "administrative management" to "office management," the belief being that the former more accurately describes the content and importance of supplying information by processing papers and the contributions of such efforts to an enterprise.

Any attempt to justify one major activity as the most important in an enterprise is purely academic. Actually, all the major activities are needed. For example, production requires sales, financing gives rise to paper work, personnel assists production, and paper work expedites sales efforts. Our interest here is organization in the management of the office; and the vital concept for our purpose is to remember that office work is done to help fulfill other major functions—it is not performed apart from them. Production activities such as cutting, sewing, machining, assembling, painting, drying, and packing are assisted by the work of the office. Likewise, typical sales activities such as merchandising, analysis of markets, and selling efforts are helped by the office. And the same is true of finance and personnel, for many records and papers are needed in each.

ORGANIZATIONAL CONTENT AND PLACEMENT OF THE OFFICE

The questions can now be asked: "What activities should be included in the office?" and "Where should the office organizational unit be placed in the organization of the entire enterprise?" The answers must be known so that organizational relationships can be identified both within the office itself and between the office and major organizational units of the enterprise. These relationships can be termed (1) intradepartmental— among the activities making up the office, and (2) interdepartmental— among the office and other major organizational units of the enterprise. The interdepartmental viewpoint is especially helpful because it emphasizes the facilitating and service aspects of office work.

Actually, to designate an organizational unit as "the office" can be confusing, for it is likely neither to be in one location nor to include all office activities. To reiterate, office work is not an activity in and of itself; it is a part of and employed in almost every function. Office work contributes information needed in performing the major functions of production, sales, finance, personnel, and other functions, such as engineering, research, and purchasing, which are necessary in a particular organization.

Logically, from the organizing point of view, the required office work should be located where it can be performed at lowest cost, assist best in achieving the stated objectives, and supply the highest service to those using it. This is determined by giving consideration to a number of factors, of which the following are important:

1. *Type and nature of the enterprise.* The content and the placement of the office function are affected greatly by the dominance of the production, sales, finance, or personnel activities. If the enterprise is primarily one for production—a large manufacturer, for example, selling

its entire output to several large buyers—the office unit probably will be of relatively small importance. However, in a predominantly financial enterprise, the work will be of relatively great importance. To illustrate, in a bank or insurance company, office work is usually of much greater importance than it is in a manufacturing company. Likewise, in a governmental enterprise, the office unit normally occupies a position relatively high in the organizational structure.

2. *Importance attached to office work.* If top managers of an enterprise recognize the work of the office as of relatively high significance, the tendency will probably be to bring it together into one organizational unit and place this unit high in the organizational structure. But if office work is considered minor, although necessary, it probably will be performed by the department needing it and coordinated as completely as possible with the primary activities of the respective department.

3. *Degree of office mechanization used.* Up to a certain level, the adoption of office machines has small effect upon the organization structure. But when machines capable of processing huge quantities of work or of performing work historically handled by several departments are adopted, the result organizationwise is to consolidate the work, shrink the department, combine departments, and change the organizational framework. This can readily be seen in the case of computers and their impact upon office organizing. Significant changes also take place when high-speed accounting machines, punched-card machines, automatic typewriters, and duplicating machines are installed.

4. *Extent of centralization of office functions.* Since office work occurs throughout the entire enterprise, from the president's office to the lowest-paid clerk, it is possible to have it performed in dispersed locations, under the jurisdiction of the unit in which it arises. When this practice is followed, the office function is dispersed and either combined with, or made subordinate to, other organizational units. In its fullest application, this dispersion extends to the smallest and lowest organizational unit of the enterprise. In contrast, a directly opposite arrangement might be used. In this case, the office work is fully concentrated and is placed in the hands of a single executive who is completely responsible for all office activities in the organization.

These two conditions, however, are extreme. From a practical viewpoint, seldom is either used. An intermediate or modified arrangement between these two extremes is commonly followed:

1. Office work is located and performed by major departments, and each department head is fully responsible for the office activities in his own department.

2. Office work is distributed among all departments, but one person is placed in charge of this office work in order to achieve reasonable coordination.

3. Certain office work is centralized in one unit and placed under one manager. The remaining office work is performed in the unit in which it arises and is supervised by the regular department head of that unit. This arrangement is quite popular. It is interpreted in different arrangements, and the more common of these are discussed in the following paragraphs.

THE OFFICE SERVICES ARRANGEMENT

Office services include corresponding, report writing, mail and office communicating services, duplicating, calculating, filing, and records retention. They are frequently included in an office organizational unit and placed under the "office services manager" or, in some cases, the "office manager." However, all these services are not always centralized, the notable exceptions being corresponding, report writing, calculating, and filing. Furthermore, even when all these services are referred to as being centralized, they are only partially so—some of certain services being located in various units throughout the entire organization structure.

The adoption of an "office services" unit arrangement means that the manager in charge of office work has a dual managerial task. First, he should manage the services unit; and second, since office work is being performed in various other units in which it arises, he should counsel with the executives of these various units and help them accomplish their office work in the best manner. This second task is of paramount importance and in many respects establishes the true status of the office manager in any organization structure. Actually, it is identifying what office work is and demonstrating to other managers in the organization how best to accomplish this type of work, in essence providing the office work viewpoint to all managers of the enterprise. All use office work; hence, help in how to use it effectively constitutes a real service. Figure 1, top left illustration, shows graphically the office services arrangement.

THE SYSTEMS AND PROCEDURES ARRANGEMENT

As recognition that the "systems approach" can increase office efficiency, many companies have established an organization unit to facilitate this particular viewpoint and effort. The exact format, content, location, and authority of this organizational unit varies considerably from company to company. For our purposes here, it is identified as the "systems and procedures department"; but other common titles are

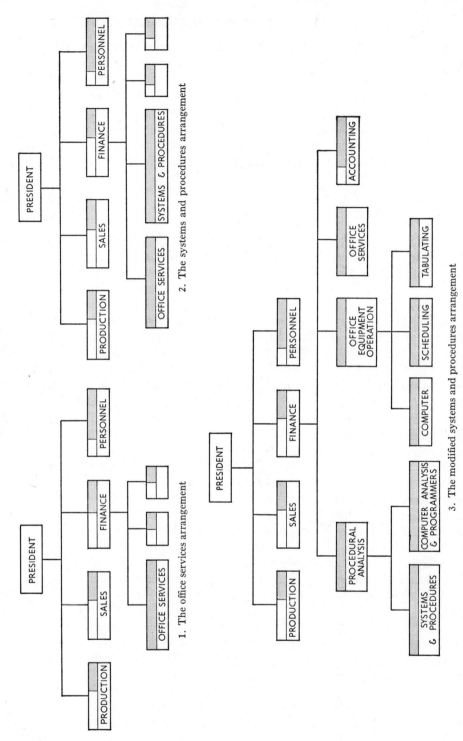

1. The office services arrangement

2. The systems and procedures arrangement

3. The modified systems and procedures arrangement

FIG. 1. Various organizing arrangements of office work with reference to the entire enterprise. The shaded areas approximate the relative amount of office work.

systems department, procedures department, methods department, or business services department. Probably none of these titles identifies completely and clearly the work performed. For discussion purposes, we have assumed that this unit is subordinate to the major unit of finance. It is also common to subordinate it to the controller's office. Any or all of the following activities may be included in the systems and procedures unit: (1) office systems, procedures, and methods design and implementation—to determine and use the proper office operations, their best sequence, and the manner of performance to get the office work accomplished efficiently; (2) computer analysis and programming to operate the computer; (3) analysis of other office machines and equipment in order to advise what type of machine or equipment should be used for a specific type of office work under the prescribed conditions; (4) office layout and working conditions—to recommend the most effective arrangement of office facilities and the physical surroundings to supply; (5) office standards—to relate useful levels of performance or frames of reference in order to evaluate achievement; and (6) office work simplification—to point out ways to eliminate waste of all kinds and get the office work out more effectively. The systems and procedures arrangement is illustrated by the top right illustration of Figure 1.

THE MODIFIED SYSTEMS AND PROCEDURES ARRANGEMENT

As computer usage has increased, some companies have adopted what might be termed a modified systems and procedures arrangement. Here the procedural analysis for systems and computer facilitation is separated from the implementation of the machines. Experience has shown that above certain levels or volumes of activity, the work of computer and other office machine scheduling and usage are best segregated from the design and analysis functions for these machines. The bottom illustration of Figure 1 shows this arrangement. Note that the procedural analysis section includes (1) *all* systems and procedures work throughout the company in one unit and (2) the work dealing with computer analysis and programming in another unit. The head of the procedural analysis section coordinates the activities of systems and procedures men and that of the computer analytical personnel. Also, observe that the computer analysts and programmers make up *one* unit in order to maintain close organizational ties between these related activities.

THE ADMINISTRATIVE SERVICES ORGANIZATIONAL ARRANGEMENT

Primarily because office automation has increased and especially as the strong trend toward computers has taken place, the organization of those supplying information has been modified to better meet current needs. The concept of an "administrative services" organizational unit on par with other major units of an enterprise has developed and is winning favor. This arrangement places most of the office work under a single administrator. The top illustration of Figure 2 shows the administrative services arrangement. For illustrative purposes only, the units under administrative services are shown as systems and procedures, machine operation, and office services. Observe that the efforts of designing how the work will be accomplished (systems and procedures) is segregated from that of implementation (machine operation). Also, that analyzing and programming essential for computer usage is concentrated in a separate unit from that of the efforts designing the means to be used for the paper work in general. Modern electronic machines make it feasible to handle a large part of the paper work of an enterprise in one organizational unit. However, even under the administrative services arrangement, some office work is performed in other major units, simply because it is easier, more convenient, and of greater service to perform some of the office work in these other units.

Having an administrative services unit is a departure from the initial and still widely used arrangement of having the office unit include the computer group and the entire unit under the finance or the controller major unit. The main reason for favoring the finance vice-president or the controller was that he could move with freedom across organizational lines, was already associated with office machines and procedures, and the work to be done by the computer—notably payroll, accounts payable, and accounts receivable—was already his responsibility. But as experience was gained and applications broadened, the automatic assignment of computer stewardship to the finance executive or controller was questioned. It was reasoned, and quite correctly, that the office organization should take into account:

1. *The objectives of the computer usage.* Is reduction of office cost or improvement of managerial information primary? Can a computer assist and take an increasing role in the overall management process of the enterprise?

2. *The scope of the applications.* The broader the range of applications, the stronger the reasons for a separate administrative services unit. For example, if the usage is broadened in scope from processing of routine data to sophisticated management decision making, the chances are that a separate unit will be the more effective organizational vehicle.

3. *The organizational strength of the finance executive or the controller.* It is readily apparent that the man in charge of an activity determines its contribution and importance. The manager should compre-

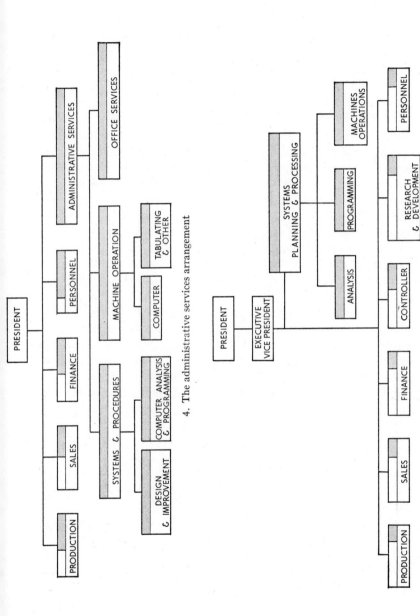

4. The administrative services arrangement

5. The top staff administrative services arrangement

FIG. 2. Two administrative services organizational arrangements each of which provide top recognition and status to office work efforts. The shaded areas approximate the relative amount of office work.

hend the tremendous contribution of better information, creating effective systems and procedures, and harnessing the huge potential of the computer. In addition, competence in working effectively with, and securing action from, major executives and having the support and confidence of top management are essential. In many instances, the finance executive or the controller meets these requirements fully while in other instances there appears to be an inadequacy.

THE TOP STAFF ADMINISTRATIVE SERVICES ARRANGEMENT

The bottom illustration of Figure 2 represents a simplified form of a large enterprise with an extensive informational services unit and large-scale electronic data processing. Responsibility for all this work is fixed in a department executive reporting directly to the executive vice-president. This department serves as a service group to all other departments including the vice-president of finance or the controller. Also, the department head has charge of small paper work staffs maintained by some of the major departments such as sales and research and development. These small staffs are not shown in the figure.

This arrangement permits company-wide coordination of all paper work systems. It identifies informational activities with the top management and enhances the enlistment and support of department heads. The informational needs can be determined objectively without predisposition to a particular means or solution. Either manual, semimechanical, or complete computer application can be evolved and installed after all alternatives have been carefully evaluated. An avowed goal of this arrangement is to improve the quality of information made available to management members.

CENTRALIZATION AND OFFICE ORGANIZING

"Centralization of office activities" means the physical concentration of such activities into a single group, with the management over them vested in one person. For example, in centralized filing, all filing work for an entire office is done by a filing section and managed by a filing chief. Centralization is concentration.

Actually, the concept of centralization can be considered from the viewpoint of (1) physical location or (2) management. This, in turn, permits four possibilities, namely, (1) physical location centralized and management centralized, (2) physical location not centralized and management centralized, (3) physical location not centralized and management not centralized, and (4) physical location centralized and management not centralized. Illustrations of these four possibilities, along with comments for each, are shown in Figure 3.

A key consideration in office organizing is the degree of office work centralization from the management viewpoint which is adopted. As already indicated, the degree of centralization of "office services" varies among different enterprises; by no means do all enterprises have a department akin to the systems and procedures department, and relatively few have some form of an administrative services department. Equipment analysis, for example, may be handled by the executive handling the particular function for which the equipment will be used; likewise, the executive of the operating department may have charge of standards

POSSIBILITY 1

PHYSICAL LOCATION : CENTRALIZED
MANAGEMENT :   CENTRALIZED

POSSIBILITY 2

PHYSICAL LOCATION: NOT CENTRALIZED
MANAGEMENT :   CENTRALIZED

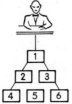

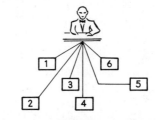

COMMENT: COMMON CONCEPT
OF CENTRALIZATION

COMMENT: COMMON BUT SOMETIMES
NOT FULLY COMPREHENDED
AS A TYPE OF CENTRALIZATION

POSSIBILITY 3

PHYSICAL LOCATION: NOT CENTRALIZED
MANAGEMENT :   NOT CENTRALIZED

POSSIBILITY 4

PHYSICAL LOCATION: CENTRALIZED
MANAGEMENT: NOT CENTRALIZED

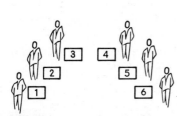

COMMENT:
SERIES OF INDIVIDUAL UNITS.
ACTUALLY NO CENTRALIZATION
CONCEPT EXISTS

COMMENT:
RELATIVELY RARE CONCEPT OF
CENTRALIZATION - LITTLE USED

FIG. 3.   The four possibilities of centralization.

applying to paper work in his unit. A computer may be located solely within one department such as research and development and this arrangement is satisfactory providing the single department has sufficient work to require the full time of the computer. The particular organizational pattern followed depends upon many factors, but the degree of centralization is vital and merits further comment.

EVALUATION OF OFFICE CENTRALIZATION

The current trend appears to be toward centralization. Office automation, use of computers, consolidating fragmented clerical functions, and taking organizational measures to stop the spiraling of overhead costs are among the major reasons for this trend. A suggested approach to determine the feasibility of centralization of office work is discussed in Chapter 9. Specifically, the advantages of office centralization include:

1. Flexibility is given the organization. Work peak loads can be readily handled, office machinery utilized fully, and the effects of labor shortages reduced to a minimum.

2. Equitable wage schedules are fostered. The measurement of office output is encouraged, and comparisons of wages for similar work are possible.

3. Training of office employees is expedited. New employees can be added to centralized groups without seriously affecting the operations of the group. The retraining of old employees for new jobs is also well adapted to a centralized type of organization.

4. Methods of office operation can be applied uniformly and quickly. Standards common to several organizational units can be established.

5. Cost of performing office work is decreased. Supervisory costs are lowered, the costs of investment and maintenance of machines are lowered, and the amount of floor space is frequently reduced.

6. Labor specialization is practiced. Employees become highly efficient and are continuously employed on work necessitating their highest individual skill and ability.

On the other hand, there are many who feel that better results are obtained from a noncentralized, or decentralized, organizational arrangement of the office work. To substantiate their view they point out that:

1. Much office work is confidential and should be handled by the unit in which this confidential trust is placed.

2. The work is performed by those who may not be familiar with the detailed requirements. Minor changes and corrections cannot be made on the spot.

3. Effective planning and controlling are difficult to exercise since the executives most familiar with the use and purpose of the paper work are not near at hand.

4. Work is done without regard for urgency or importance to the individual office unit. Delays may take place. The efficiency of each unit may be hampered.

5. Costs may increase due to nonproductive transporting and handling time required.

6. Employees of a "generalist" nature are not developed. Some versatile persons with overall viewpoints are essential in all enterprises.

It should also be added that for a noncentralized office arrangement to provide satisfactory results, certain organizational requirements should be met. These include (1) a clear understanding and agreement among all management personnel of the office goals and the basic policies to be followed, (2) written statements covering office work decision making to be performed by nonoffice management members, (3) an effective reporting to the office manager of what decisions concerning paper work are being made by nonoffice management members, and (4) a follow-up and postdecision audit should be maintained. When such practices exist, sound decentralized decisions can be made and an effective organization maintained.

THE OFFICE ACTIVITIES

For instructional purposes, it is helpful to enumerate the various office activities that can exist in an enterprise in order to afford a panorama of office work. As indicated above, the location and arrangement of office activities assume a variety of patterns and relations. The following is not intended to represent any particular office or serve as a specific recommendation.

The many and various office activities, segregated by six major divisions, include:

1. Office automation (deals with utilization of computer and of SDA, source data automation).
   1.1 Computer analysis and programming.
   1.2 Operation of computer.
   1.3 Determination and application of SDA.
   1.4 Filing and storage of media—punched cards, punched tape, magnetic tape, and so forth.
2. Office services (includes activities commonly thought of in reference to office work).

    2.1 Correspondence and office reports.
       2.11 Stenographic and typing work.
       2.12 Billing.
    2.2 Communicating services.
       2.21 Mail and messenger services.
       2.22 Telephone and telegraph.
    2.3 Calculating.
       2.31 Data for reports.
       2.32 Statistical data.
    2.4 Filing.
    2.5 Records retention.

3. Office planning (encompasses activities dealing with what office work will be performed, when, where, and how).
    3.1 Determination of objectives, policies, systems, procedures, and methods.
       3.11 Routines and flow of office work.
       3.12 Design and use of office forms.
    3.2 Use of office machines and equipment.
    3.3 Research.

4. Physical facilities of the office (consist of activities pertaining to the securing, using, and maintaining of physical factors needed for performing office work).
    4.1 Location and arrangements.
       4.11 Office layouts.
       4.12 Office lighting, ventilating, and noise control.
    4.2 Purchasing.
       4.21 Office machines.
       4.22 Office furniture and equipment.
          4.221 Desks, chairs, and filing cabinets.
       4.23 Office forms and supplies.
          4.231 Storage and issuance of same.

5. Office controlling (consists of activities of work measurement and comparison to see that office work is performed as planned).
    5.1 Operational analysis.
       5.11 Office standards.
          5.111 Office systems, procedures, and methods.
          5.112 Office forms.
          5.113 Office machines, furniture, and equipment.
       5.12 Office work simplification.
       5.13 Office work measurement.
       5.14 Office manuals.
    5.2 Work and cost control.

       5.21 Routing and scheduling.

       5.22 Peak work load handling.

       5.23 Cost analysis and office budgets.

6. Office personnel (includes employee motivation and relationships with fellow employees, with the job, and with the public of the enterprise).

  6.1 Office employment.

      6.11 Recruitment, selection, and placement.

          6.111 Interviews, tests, and references.

      6.12 Transfers, promotions, and terminations.

  6.2 Salary administration.

      6.21 Job description and evaluation.

      6.22 Job performance rating.

  6.3 Office training.

  6.4 Welfare.

      6.41 Grievances.

      6.42 Suggestion system.

      6.43 Office safety.

      6.44 Office employee benefits—pensions and hospital insurance.

CHAPTER TWO

ESTABLISHING PROPER

WORK DIVISIONS AND JOB

ASSIGNMENTS

*The talent of success is nothing more than doing what you can do well;
and doing well whatever you do, without a thought of fame.*
—Henry Wadsworth Longfellow

IT IS implied in the previous chapter that for organizing to take place, work is divided, forming clusters of tasks, and people are assigned to these tasks. The resulting "work division–people assigned" segments provide the nuclei of organization units. How to divide the work and the important considerations in assigning people to vitalize the organization are discussed in this chapter. We start with work division because, in the great majority of cases, this is the superior approach. A manager must coordinate what is done, not who is doing it. Also, the work is relatively permanent, it changes less frequently than the interests and abilities of personnel. Furthermore, to formulate organization units primarily on the basis of personnel often results in unusual combinations of duties that are difficult to manage and for which the securing of replacements is arduous. However, the "people–work" division approach is used and in some instances with outstanding success.

WORK DIVISION

There are many different means for dividing the work in office organizing, including (1) by function, (2) by process, (3) by customer, (4) by product, (5) by territory, and (6) by project. An organizer can use any means he desires, and commonly several means are employed in the same organization structure. What best helps to achieve the objective should be used. In a bank, for example, for the top levels, functions may be used; whereas the loan department may be divided by customer—loans to manufacturers of plastics, chemicals, and paper; loans to manufacturers of food processors and package machines; or by product—commercial loans or personal loans. Office work division by territory is common for offices designed to serve sales organizations. The territory divisions constitute the main segments of the sales organizational structure, and the offices serving such organizations are likewise segregated and located throughout the country. Work division by project in office organization has been used very little as of now. It utilizes the idea of work division being a project or a major and complete program. Assigned to a project is a complete team which is permitted to work on the project assigned until either successful completion or an authorized termination is ordered, at which time the team is disbanded and new projects are activated with newly formed teams believed appropriate for the new work involved. Large research development agencies of government are using project organization with great success. In the future it may become an important segment of office organizing.

The most common means of departmentation is by function, which can be defined as *the normal or characteristic operation of an activity*. Filing, for example, is a function in that it is an activity which always has characteristic identities, and these identities are usually considered the proper action of filing. In management, it is common to speak of "functions," such as the function of producing, the function of selling, and the function of financing. For example, the function of producing means the normal or characteristic operation of producing goods or services. In turn, any function covering a broad scope of action such as producing can be broken up into component functions of a relatively limited scope. For producing, these component functions may include the function of designing, the function of plant layout, the function of fabricating, the function of assembling, the function of inspection, the function of production control, and the function of purchasing.

The same function may be performed by two or more people and likewise, the same person may perform two or more functions. Illustrative of the former is a group of clerks all doing the same work, for example, checking billings in a department. The latter case is illustrated by the receptionist who greets and directs visitors, opens and sorts the mail, and types letters.

EXISTENT DIVISION OF WORK

For an existent organization, data on the current work divisions as well as who performs the different tasks can be surveyed and recorded on a work distribution chart. Basically this is a spread sheet which shows, for a given time period—usually a week—the type of work and the time spent on each job by each employee in the office organization unit under review. The basic information can be obtained from the supervisor or the employees. Probably more objective data are obtained by observing each employee and recording information on his activities. However, this approach is relatively expensive.

Figure 4 shows a work distribution chart. A vertical column is used for each employee, along with one to indicate the time spent on each

OFFICE FUNCTIONS	TOTAL MAN HOURS	LOIS MILLER Unit Supervisor	MAN HOURS	BETTY HEIDT Stenographer	MAN HOURS	RUTH TOPFF Order Clerk	MAN HOURS	EDITH WRIGHT File Clerk	MAN HOURS	SYLVIA GAZEL Telephone Switch board Operator	MAN HOURS
Correspondence	54	Read and route Dictation	9 / 10	Takes dictation Transcribes	10 / 20	Types labels and materials for files	5				
Computing	32	Figures prices	3	Figures prices	2	Figures prices	15	Figures prices	12		
Filing	21					Files correspondence Finds letters in file	2 / 5	Files correspondence Finds letters in file Classifies correspondence	4 / 6 / 4		
Handling mail	26	Opens mail Time stamps mail	2 / 5	Stamps mail	2	Opens mail	5	Stamps mail	4	Opens mail Stamps mail	3 / 5
Miscellaneous	67	Answers questions Answers Telephone inquiries Supervises	8 / 2 / 1	Cleans typewriter Gets supplies Arranges advertising stuffing material	1 / 2 / 3	Answers telephone inquiries	2	Errands for postage stamps and supplies Maintains tickler file for follow-ups	8 / 8	Operates switch-board	32
	200		40		40		40		40		40

FIG. 4.   Work distribution chart.

activity. The functions performed are listed in the first column on the left. This chart gives a graphic, overall picture of the work done and the work divisions in effect. In addition, it reveals the relative amounts of time put on each office function and the extent of work division. From the "people assigned" viewpoint, the chart shows what skills are required, whether special skills are being wasted, whether too many employees are performing the same function, and whether an employee is doing too many unrelated tasks.

INDIVIDUAL JOB CONTENT

From the organizing viewpoint, individual job content is the contribution to the objective made by the individual performing the particular job. The activities assigned or the individual job content can be viewed as what the employee is required to perform because of the organizational position and relationship occupied in the organization structure.

Effective organizing requires that each employee have definite tasks that he understands, can perform, and that encourage his personal development. When these requirements are met and the necessary physical facilities and adequate supervision are provided, the individual is in an ideal work situation where real accomplishments are possible.

The division of work to be done must be carried out to the individual job level. That is, the department functions must be divided ultimately into jobs for each individual. Unless this is done, the managerial work of organizing is incomplete, and the group of people connected with the enterprise cannot perform as a whole or contribute with a unity of action.

JOB SPECIALIZATION

All organizing requires some specialization. Most managers agree that no one person can do everything equally well. The need for allocating total work and capitalizing upon what a person can perform best have resulted in job specialization. Complex work is divided into relatively simple components, each accomplished effectively by employees specializing in that single operation or in a group of similar operations. The question is not whether to have job specialization but to what extent job specialization should be carried. In organizing, the office manager must decide this question as exemplified by determining the work makeup of each organizational unit and what is done by each member of that unit. Too many and too varied tasks for one employee are generally avoided. On the other hand, a job of very limited scope is not used, presumably to minimize the problem of monotony and lack of employee interest in his work.

In some enterprises, where the office organizing has utilized job specialization to a great degree, provisions such as job rotation, "music while you work," rest periods, and keeping the employee informed of all major enterprise operations have been adopted to maintain high morale and to make the organizational structure effective. For the most part, the degree of specialization has not been questioned. However, in some companies, an attempt to broaden the job scope has been advanced. This is commonly referred to as *job enlargement*. These efforts have given surprising results, such as reduced office costs, improved quality of work, better teamwork, and lower absenteeism. These results, which must be interpreted carefully, indicate that there are both economic and social limits to job specialization. The degree and form of job specialization to follow presumably depend upon the type of office work and the individual doing it. More specific information is needed to derive definite recommendations, but it appears that the prevalent ideas concerning job specialization should be modified.

WORK DIVISION ARRANGEMENTS

Generally speaking, work divisions for the top level of an organizational structure are made on the basis of functions. Divisions for the intermediate levels usually are either by type of product, by customer, or by territory. Common at the lower office organizational levels are work divisions by any of these three arrangements: (1) serial, (2) parallel, and (3) unit assembly. Work division by product, customer, or territory is self-explanatory; but further discussion of the serial, parallel, and unit assembly is warranted.

In the serial arrangement, the work division is extended to a series of small tasks, each task being performed by a specialist in that particular type of work. Moving progressively from task to task, the work advances until completed. The serial arrangement is the same basic plan as the familiar factory assembly line, commonly found in production plants. In some quarters, the term "production line basis" is used to describe the serial arrangement in the office. "Consecutive handling" adequately describes this arrangement.

The parallel arrangement permits a series of needed and separate tasks to be performed by one individual or a work team. The employee or employees, as the case might be, do not specialize in performing one task but gain proficiency in accomplishing several tasks. Frequently, the tasks are related, but this is not necessary. To implement the parallel arrangement, the total work is divided into two or more major parts, and each part is assigned to an employee or group of employees. The basis for dividing the work into parts can be any of many factors, for example, by letter of the alphabet, number, territory, type of merchandise, or major subject. From the individual's viewpoint, the scope of the work is relatively large under the parallel arrangement. The term "concurrent handling" can be used to identify this arrangement.

The unit assembly arrangement provides for different employees to perform different work steps upon the same work items at the same time. It can be termed "simultaneous handling." Each step is done by a specialist in his particular type of work. Coordination of the various tasks is a prime requirement under this arrangement, for the separate tasks usually do not require identical times to perform. The unit assembly arrangement can be thought of as a cross-blending between the serial and the parallel arrangement.

Figure 5 shows these three basic arrangements in graphic form. The

SERIAL
(CONSECUTIVE
HANDLING)

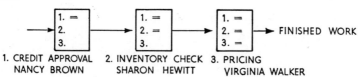

1. CREDIT APPROVAL   2. INVENTORY CHECK   3. PRICING
   NANCY BROWN   SHARON HEWITT   VIRGINIA WALKER

PARALLEL
(CONCURRENT
HANDLING)

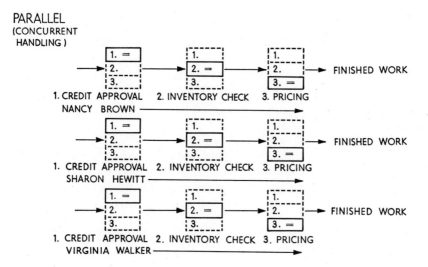

1. CREDIT APPROVAL   2. INVENTORY CHECK   3. PRICING
   NANCY BROWN

1. CREDIT APPROVAL   2. INVENTORY CHECK   3. PRICING
   SHARON HEWITT

1. CREDIT APPROVAL   2. INVENTORY CHECK   3. PRICING
   VIRGINIA WALKER

UNIT ASSEMBLY
(SIMULTANEOUS
HANDLING)

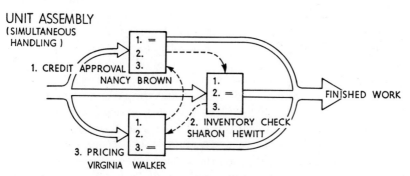

1. CREDIT APPROVAL
NANCY BROWN

2. INVENTORY CHECK
SHARON HEWITT

3. PRICING
VIRGINIA WALKER

FINISHED WORK

FIG. 5.   Illustrating the serial, parallel, and unit assembly arrangements of work division.

work considered pertains to the handling of customers' orders and consists of three separate operations, including (1) credit approval, (2) inventory check, and (3) pricing. Assume a work force of three employees, Nancy Brown, Sharon Hewitt, and Virginia Walker. The serial arrangement is shown at the top of the figure. For simplicity, each separate operation has been considered a separate task, and one employee has been assigned to each task. In contrast, the parallel arrangement is shown at the center of Figure 5. In this illustration, the total customer order-handling work has been divided into three parts that parallel each other. Each part consists of all three separate tasks of the work, that is, credit approval, inventory check, and pricing. As illustrated, employee Nancy Brown performs all three tasks or operations, and so do each of the other two employees, Sharon Hewitt and Virginia Walker. The bottom illustration of Figure 5 shows the unit assembly arrangement. Here, specialization is practiced by each employee, but the work sequence is not identical for each item. Nancy Brown performs credit approval; while at the same time, Sharon Hewitt performs inventory check, and Virginia Walker does pricing.

WHAT ARRANGEMENT TO USE

Like many other practices, the question of whether to use the serial, parallel, or unit assembly arrangement cannot be fully answered by a "Yes" or "No." Normally, for any given office, the tendency is toward the prevalence of one, but seldom will it be used exclusively. Individual circumstances govern, with consideration given to cost, employees' interest in their jobs, quality of work, preferences of managers and employees, and the overall objectives.

More specifically, the serial arrangement of work division requires a sufficient work quantity of a particular type to keep an employee fully occupied in its performance. Quantity and specialization are close "buddies." Also, mechanization tends toward a serial arrangement. Most office machines handle a large volume of work, and their cost usually requires a high percentage of utilization throughout the workday. In some instances, the job content is so complex and the tasks so heterogeneous that some breakdown in the work is necessary to acquire and maintain employees for the work. When this is the case, the serial arrangement is usually followed. In addition, some office work, if performed by one employee, would incur a sizable loss of time in shifting from one operator to another. For example, a job consisting of typing, then calculating, followed by checking and resumption of typing, may show low efficiency. Selecting the serial plan frequently follows when the skill needed is of a special type, due to scarcity or the amount of training that can economically be provided. It is usually not feasible to dilute the efforts of the employee possessing a needed skill in a specialty. An expert in operating punched-card equipment should not type and file letters as a part of her regular job duties. Another condition normally suggesting the adoption of the serial arrangement is when great uniformity in handling certain portions of the office work is required. The signing of checks and bank drafts can be cited as an illustration.

In contrast, the parallel arrangement is usually followed when better work performance appears to be associated with a complete understanding and handling of the particular subject matter. An overcharge in a billing to a complaining customer might best be handled in its entirety by one employee. Furthermore, when the "start to finish" period for the work performance must be reduced, the parallel arrangement may be superior. Under this pattern, delay in work processing, or loss in time by papers traveling from operation to operation, is avoided. Less handling and idle time generally result when the papers are processed by employees working under a parallel arrangement. In some cases, by keeping the division of work too small, an employee is deprived of helpful overall checks in the work. When this situation exists, the parallel arrangement automatically provides the solution. It should also be observed that with parallel groups performing similar cycles of work, it is possible to hold contests, compare work accomplishments of each group, and inject other competitive devices in managing the work. Such measures help stimulate high productivity. In addition, the parallel arrangement helps to eliminate duplication of efforts such as reading and checking if such is present when high specialization is followed. Under the parallel pattern, one employee familiarizes herself with the contents of the paper by a single reading and a single checking. Finally, the parallel arrangement is suggested where the circumstances indicate that greater interest and enthusiasm by employees probably will be gained from having a greater variety of work in the job makeup.

The unit assembly arrangement permits work to start at an operation other than the first in the sequence of tasks. This makes it possible to start processing the work simultaneously at different operational stages. In other words, the performance of work operation No. 3 need not wait until No. 1 and No. 2 are completed. In certain situations, this is a definite advantage. Furthermore, flexibility in machine utilization and in work scheduling are provided. Usually, completed work is obtained more rapidly under the unit assembly arrangement; for this reason, it is employed for special rush and emergency work. Specialization is practiced to a great degree under this arrangement; but as stated above, sometimes the coordination of the individual work processing poses a difficult problem.

JOB ANALYSIS

Job analysis is a formal means of determining the job content. It can be defined as follows: *Job analysis is the process of critically examining the components of a job, both separately and in relation to the whole, in order to determine all the operations and duties.* In short, job analysis deals with facts about jobs and what is required for competent performance. Typical of data included are the forms and materials handled, the equipment and machines used, the methods utilized, the frequency of the operations, the amounts and kinds of skill required, and the degree of concentration needed. Such information is extremely useful in management because (1) the scope of the job becomes definite, (2) the identity becomes fixed, and (3) definite association between job title and content is established.

Job analysis is customarily and quite correctly thought of as an activity logically a part of personnel activities because it is basic in the performance of many personnel department functions. For example, job analysis is the basis for determining the relative worth, compensation-wise, of jobs; it facilitates hiring and placing, can be used for formulating training needs, and serves to identify promotions and transfers. While these are truly personnel functions, job analysis is included here because it does identify the job and its content, and is pertinent to this discussion dealing with organizing. As already pointed out, really effective and complete organizing work requires specific work divisions at the individual level. Job analysis helps supply this requirement.

OBTAINING JOB ANALYSIS DATA

In the case of new work or a new organizational unit, the manager doing the organizing must decide the characteristics of the newly created job or jobs. In a going office, however, three methods of securing job analysis data are possible: (1) interview and observation, (2) conferences, and (3) questionnaires. For the first method, the analyst goes to the employee, asks questions about the job, and observes what the content of the job is. While this method is satisfactory for office jobs, it is probably most popular for factory jobs. In the second method, the employee is called into conference and verbally describes his job to the analyst, who records the information. This method usually requires more time than the others, takes the employee from his job, and may interfere with the work routine. In the third method, a questionnaire is sent to the employee, who fills in the information. This method is used in cases where the employees can intelligently handle clerical details and are more or less accustomed to paper work. It is commonly used for most office work. The federal government has employed this procedure successfully for over 50 years. Frequently the questionnaires are supplemented with short observations and interviews, especially for the more important jobs.

Whatever method is adopted, it is advisable to secure within practical limits as much information as possible about each job. It is usually better to have too much than too little data. Commonly the data are recorded on a prepared form, called a job analysis report. This form serves as a reminder to answer definite questions and thereby secure all the needed facts, so that no part of the job is overlooked. It also expedites recording the data in a standardized manner, thus making it easier to handle and interpret the information. Figure 6 shows a portion of a job analysis form.

JOB ANALYSIS

Present title of job _____ Department _____

1. What is the general purpose of this job?
2. What duties are performed in the *usual* course of the work? (Tell from where work is received, what is done with it, and where it is sent.)
3. What duties are performed only at stated intervals? (Give answers by daily, weekly, monthly, etc.)
4. In what organizational unit is this job presently located?
5. Does the job entail supervising other employees? (Explain.)
6. If there are any special training courses essential in order to perform the duties of this job satisfactorily, name them.
7. What past experience is *necessary* for a new employee to have in order to perform the duties of this job?
8. What are the *most* difficult parts of this job?
9. What are the *least* difficult parts of this job?
10. About what proportions of this job require sitting, _____%; standing, _____%; moving about, _____%?
11. What machines or other equipment are operated?
    Regularly:
    Occasionally:

FIG. 6.   Portion of questionnaire used for job analysis.

JOB DESCRIPTION

The information on the job analysis form actually describes the job. However, when this information is written in a more descriptive style, the term "job description" is frequently used. While the format used for writing these descriptions varies, they usually contain a summary of the job, the work performed, and the qualifications generally considered essential. (See Figure 7.)

JOB DESCRIPTION

DATE_____

JOB TITLE__ JUNIOR ACCOUNTANT _____GRADE__VI____CODE_____

SUMMARY:
Under general direction of Comptroller and immediate supervision of Accountant, performs general accounting duties and prepares special reports as assigned.

WORK PERFORMED:
Maintains records of cash receipts and/or disbursements, posts related subsidiary records. Posts various journal entries and adjustments, maintains record of Supply Department receipts and prepares minor financial statements.

Handles correspondence, verifies tabulations and reconciles bank statement. Assists in distributing work to temporary help, prepares monthly reports and special statements. Performs related work, such as figuring per capita and expense ratios. Operates office machines as required.

May supervise work of accounting clerks, typists for temporary periods, etc. and performs similar duties as assigned.

QUALIFICATIONS:
Normally requires three to five years' training and experience, including two years' general accounting training plus three years' company accounting experience as an Accounting Clerk.

Courtesy: J. D. Moore Organization, Park Ridge, Ill.

FIG. 7.   A job description written in an effective form.

Job descriptions are useful in the work of organizing. The duties and the lines of authority, if any, are clearly set forth. Job descriptions also help bring about better understanding within an enterprise because they point out the qualifications required of an employee on the particular job, help in selecting persons best fitted for the requirements of the job, and assist in acquainting the new employee with his job.

Current practice tends to use the terms "job description," "job statement," and "job title" to identify progressively contracting descriptions of the job. A job statement is used to furnish a quick picture of the job. To illustrate, in Figure 8, the job content of "programming manager"

Programming Manager: Reports to director of procedural analysis. Supervises administrative assistant programmer. Is responsible for planning and organizing all programming activities for the computer; maintaining essential records of the programming department; directing, motivating, and evaluating personnel; and participating in the planning of computer usage.

FIG. 8.   Job statement of programming manager.

is condensed to a single paragraph. A job title is simply a common name for a job. However, job titles are commonly inadequate to identify a job satisfactorily. For example, the title "secretary" is used to identify jobs of different makeup, as illustrated by the two job statements in Figure 9.

Secretary: Takes dictation, using shorthand, and transcribes the dictated material into a neat typed format; makes appointments for executive and reminds him of them; answers and makes telephone calls; handles personal and important mail; writes routine correspondence on own initiative; maintains executive's files.

Secretary: Takes dictation, using either shorthand or a machine; transcribes dictation from either shorthand notes or a machine; interviews people coming into the office, directing to other employees those who do not warrant seeing the executive; answers and makes telephone calls.

FIG. 9.   Job titles may be identical, but the respective job statements may differ.

The title plus the job content are necessary for accurate identification. This is important in office organizing where work division and organizational unit creation must be decided.

IMPORTANCE OF PEOPLE IN ORGANIZING

As stated in the beginning of this chapter, organizing can logically start with work division, and the divisions created serve as focal areas for organizational units. In turn, the work within each organizational unit must be accomplished, directly or indirectly, by people. Up to this point, attention has been directed to the work aspect of organizing; but equally important, and in the opinion of many of greater importance, is the "people aspect" of organizing. In fact, it would be difficult to overemphasize the importance of people in organizing.

Successful organizing helps provide the means for getting effective results through people's efforts. It provides for the adequate development and placement of people. While work division and assignment are important, they are not the end objective in organizing. The main goal is to make it possible for a group of people, called employees, to work cooperatively and efficiently. The total work is segregated by functions so that each individual of the work group can perform a portion of the total work in the best possible manner. The expression "Organization is people" is trite; nevertheless, it stresses the importance of people in the work of organizing. It brings out the basic idea that people constitute the center about which revolve the organizational concepts of the work to be done, the authority, and the work environment.

In the final analysis, the organization structure is a tool—it provides the grouping of specific activities and of people for the purpose of applying management. Work is accomplished by people or machines operated by people. Organizing does not accomplish any work objective; it must be implemented with people. Hence, one of the biggest jobs of a manager is to form or maintain an organization structure which permits the proper placement and the development of employees. Some claim that almost any organization structure will prove satisfactory as long as the right people are operating it. Others lay great stress on the proper division of work and relationships. No doubt, both are important. However, the point here is that people are vital in organizing; they can make or break any organization structure.

It follows, therefore, that a sound organization structure is necessary for effective employee performance. This is true because organizing deals with and sets forth such basic issues as what is to be done and by whom, and who decides what. This view of organizing has been compared to that of writing the story for a motion-picture film. It sets the stage and predetermines what is to take place. How well it takes place, i.e., the quality of the motion picture, depends in great measure upon the actors— the personnel element.

Personnel has a decidedly marked effect upon the structure of an organization. When, for example, the ratio of skilled to unskilled employees is high, the pattern of the organizational structure might be far different from that for one where the ratio is low. The reason for this, in part, is the relative importance of supervision and the placement of different functions at different levels in the two structures.

Organizing affects and is affected by the human side of group activities.

The sought-for coordination among different activities is more correctly stated as the coordination among *the employees* performing the different activities. After all, the work is divided so that it can be accomplished by the group. How effectively the various members of the group work together as a team toward achieving the objective is the paramount consideration.

MANAGER'S ATTITUDE AND ORGANIZING

Organizing reflects a manager's attitude and thinking in that it reveals the understanding of a manager for the essentiality of the human element and how this resource is to be regarded. Just allocating the work, assigning employees to neatly conceived endeavors, and granting carefully defined authority to selected persons is insufficient. The people assigned to certain tasks and the creation of certain working relation among themselves must be handled with great care. There is genuine skill in having logical work divisions tie in respectively with an adequate consideration for who is to do each respective component of work.

An office manager implements regard for the human element in his organizing work by recognizing and appreciating the value, as well as the limitations, of his employees. This is not a one-shot proposition but a continuing, ever searching effort to keep up to date on how the employees available to him can best be brought together to work toward a common goal. The supervisor in charge of the mail room, for example, reflects from the human-element viewpoint the office manager's thinking, organization-wise, of the supervisor's value, including his strong and weak points for his particular supervisory job. The job content, a result of work division, is presumably what the office manager thinks it ought to be; likewise, the authority granted is what the office manager thinks it ought to be—all or at least a big portion of it is with reference to the office manager's human-element evaluation of the supervisor. In this sense, it is sometimes said that an organization structure reflects the shadow of its manager. However, it appears more appropriate to state that an organization structure *reflects the light or understanding* of its manager.

Concentration on men's strengths pays organizational dividends. A manager holding firm convictions about an employee's abilities to perform the work competently tends to instill confidence in the employee and develops his will to do successful work. At the same time, the manager must realize that not all men can do all things. To assume otherwise can lead to disaster in his organizing. Yet, by proper managerial motivation, leadership, and lifting a man's vision to higher planes, the common man can be stimulated to achieve uncommon things.

However, the office manager who experiences the greatest success in organizing is a realist and accepts people available to him for what they really are. He recognizes that most organizational structures, and particularly the area of which he is a part, are the result of many decisions which took into account various considerations, some of which were controversial and contained imponderables. He also realizes that organizing is a "give and take" proposition between what is to be done and who is assigned to do it. Essentially, it has a compromise characteristic. The chief criterion, however, is to get the work accomplished adequately and maintain a continuity of satisfactory work achievement.

ORGANIZING AND SOCIAL IMPLICATIONS

There is a strong "rational" feature about formal organizing. It is designed, the components are purposely related, and jobs within it are carefully defined. The justification for such activities is that to do otherwise would be wasteful and haphazard. On the other hand, there is the question whether this "rational" characteristic restricts individual creativity and initiative. Does it fully meet social as well as economic needs?

Superior organizing releases potentials, creates opportunities, and stimulates the growth of its members. Most superiors want neither weak subordinates nor those clearly more capable than they. The demand is for obedient conformists who "follow the rules," do their jobs well, and handle the emergencies satisfactorily. Too rigid or too rational an organization structure may encourage passive short-time prospective employees who value only their immediate abilities. They may obtain little psychological satisfaction from their work, and to satisfy most of their human needs they may go outside the organization. In such a situation the employee may even develop an attitude that he is paid for the dissatisfactions he experiences.

What is the answer? How can both economic and social needs be met? You cannot have all employees totally independent and actively pursuing what goals their respective social needs suggest. This would make for a very difficult situation—something like "all fleas and no dog." But it is reasonable to relate organization goals with those of the individual employee. To the degree that these goals are compatible, the employee attains personal satisfaction in achieving the organization's goal. Also, social needs vary among individuals and, fortunately, the organization requires different kinds of jobs and relationships so that it appears feasible to attain satisfactory combinations of individual needs and jobs. In addition, many managers feel that the answer lies in decreasing the dependency and submissiveness of the employee by providing him with greater responsibility and a larger scope of job. The need is for "bigger" jobs and less specialized and narrow small jobs. Finally, required is greater recognition of the fact that organizing provides a facility through which employees join together to support efforts of truly competent leaders and for more productive efforts benefiting others as well as themselves. So called "loners" such as writers, artists, and composers can be viewed as achieving significant accomplishments mainly by working alone, but their works are known and perpetuated through organizations. Were it not for these organizations, the loners and their creations would sink into obscurity.

CHALLENGE OF ORGANIZATION AND PEOPLE TO MANAGERS

A major challenge of organization and people is to integrate fully the work being done by the people of the various units into a cooperative and coordinated whole. This sounds fairly simple, but acquiring it in actual practice is a different story. People are not entirely unpredictable, yet they certainly cannot be considered the same as machines. Based on available knowledge, the intricacies of the human mind are far more difficult to understand than the chemical reaction of several compounds. Consider, for example, an individual working as a member of a group. He is an individual but, at the same time, is affected by the group. If he were removed from the group and analyzed, the investigative results would have to be greatly qualified because he is not the same person he was when integrated into his organizational unit.

Another and perhaps eternal challenge is to develop a favorable organizational climate in which people are stimulated and permitted to grow. Environment is among the strongest influences to which an employee is exposed. Every organization provides environmental stimuli that affect its members, and likewise the members affect the organization. Favorable surroundings conducive to the development of a way of life, operating under the arrangement devised by organizing, must be provided. The competency of an employee may be curbed due to improper organizational relationships, or his full contribution may never be realized if he is placed in the wrong organizational unit or is not supplied the proper work environment. In the best of organizing work, there is spirit, an attitude of mind, a belief in people and what they can accomplish. A solid organization structure is not built on form or body alone.

Finally, in the work of organizing, there is the challenge of utilizing all available resources, especially people, to their utmost. The tendency is to create new authorities, new units, and to go out and get "new faces." Adequate regard should be paid the tried and true. It is not always wise to discard the traditional for something new, mainly because it is new. Good organizing requires concentration on fundamentals. From a practical viewpoint, a manager must use in the best possible manner what is available to him. At the same time, changes and newness cannot and should not be avoided, for progress demands, and is a part of, something different.

CHAPTER THREE

EMPLOYING THE CORRECT ORGANIZATIONAL RELATIONSHIPS

The work an unknown good man has done is like a vein of water flowing hidden underground, secretly making the ground green.
—*Thomas Carlyle*

THE VARIOUS organizational units made up of work divisions and people assigned to them must be related, or formally tied together, so that they provide a unified group which can operate effectively toward obtaining common objectives. Relating these units leads to the subject of authority.

Authority is the right to act or to exact action by others, within a prescribed area. With the concept of authority is associated the power to make decisions and to see that they are carried out. The compliance aspect of authority is not confined to coercion or force; more commonly, it is gained by means of persuasion and requests.

CHARACTERISTICS OF AUTHORITY

Authority has definite limitations. First of all, it must, from the management point of view, be used in conformity with the efforts to achieve the accepted goals of the organizational unit. It is not used by an office manager as his whims or wishes might suggest. Also, the use of authority is influenced by the people with whom it is being employed. The exacting of certain actions by others must be within their capacity to perform. To illustrate, trying to enforce a decision impelling an inexperi-

35

enced file clerk to operate a modern bookkeeping machine would be a ridiculous misuse of authority.

The relative position in the organization structure normally indicates the degree of authority from the formal viewpoint. But the amount of decision-making power and ultimate enforcement may be modified by the popularity or acceptance of the one in authority by the person being influenced by that authority. Managerial competence to gain enthusiastic cooperation, to acquire respect, and to inspire may be lacking despite the formal authority established by position in the organization structure. This also means that a person with little or no formal authority established by reason of his position in the structure might actually possess extensive authority due to his integrity, knowledge, and skill. In punched-card accounting, for example, others may seek suggestions from a certain individual and do what he recommends. Although the person may not be formally in charge, he actually possesses significant authority. Situations of this type may be of a temporal nature or may exist for long, continuous periods.

In many office organizational units, situations of an unusual or emergency nature arise from time to time. They may not be provided for in the regular organizational arrangement. In such circumstances, the person assuming the authority has derived it from what is called the "authority of the situation." This usually is temporary and exists until the person normally in charge assumes authority over the unusual event.

The relationship established by authority is either of two major types, (1) vertical or (2) horizontal. Vertical authority relationships are those between different organization levels and concern the superior-subordinate association. Horizontal authority relationships deal with organizational units within an organizational level and concern the manager-to-manager association within the same organization level.

Lastly, authority is dynamic. Within prescribed limits, its makeup is changed according to the specific conditions and requirements of the group or the individual. It is not always applied to the same degree or intensity. This characteristic emphasizes the manager's skill or application of his authority.

SPAN OF AUTHORITY

In writing of relationships among organizational units and the subject of authority, the question arises: How many immediate subordinates can a manager manage effectively? The number is commonly referred to as "span of control" or "span of management." For our purposes here, it is believed the term "span of authority" is appropriate and helpful.

In a given case, there is probably an optimum number of employees who should be immediately subordinate to an executive in order that most satisfactory managerial results are obtained. The number should be large enough to utilize the executive's full time and ability, yet not so large that his efforts are diluted over too wide a span. The proper span of authority depends upon many considerations.

The organizational level at which the managerial work is performed appears to be important. At the higher levels, few might report to their immediate superior; while at the lower or operative levels, many might report to one superior. Also, the type of work is important. To illustrate, a supervisor of draftsmen might adequately direct the work of 15 draftsmen, depending upon the particular type of drafting work performed. Generally speaking, a relatively broad span of authority can be used. In addition, adequate consideration must be given to whether all the immediate sub-units are of equal size and importance, whether they must be given equal attention by the supervisor, and whether the caliber of personnel requires a large or a small amount of supervision. Where the makeup of the work is fairly stable and little communication between units is required, a broad span of authority usually proves satisfactory. Furthermore, the geographical distance between activities affects the span utilized.

Some managers prefer a span numbering from four to eight. Originally, this quantity came from the military, where rapid change in plans and operations may be necessary because of enemy action. However, in business organization, the span should be determined by keeping in mind the considerations mentioned above. The number used may well be four to eight, but it need not necessarily be this amount. The span of authority appears to be increasing in many business enterprises. In some instances, successful operations are reported with spans of 10 to 12 persons at the top levels and with 20 to 25 persons at the lower levels. In the final analysis, the number of subordinates reporting to a manager should be limited to what he can effectively manage.

It is appropriate to point out that span of authority deals with the number of persons reporting to a manager, not the number of persons having access to a manager. The two can be greatly different. Also, span of authority is confined to *formal* authority relationships. Actually, in most enterprises, there are usually many informal authority relationships. These result from the existence of social interests and relationships among employees and are frequently different from the economic formal relationships established.

ORGANIZATIONAL RELATIONSHIPS AND SPAN OF AUTHORITY

It is interesting to note how the number of relationships increases as the number of persons supervised increases. First, consider a manager, M, with two supervisors, A and B. In this case, there are six relationships: M with A, M with B, and A with B, plus the reverse of each, assuming the initiative is taken by the second-named party; i.e., the additional three are A with M, B with M, and B with A. Now, assume that M increases his number of supervisors from two to three, or an increase of 50 percent. What happens to the number of relationships with which M may now be concerned? They increase from six to 18, or an increase of 200 percent. The third supervisor, C, makes for these additional 12 relationships: M with C, B with C, A with C, M with AB, M with BC, and M with AC, plus the reverse of these six relationships. This is summarized in Figure 10.

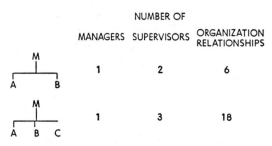

NUMBER OF

MANAGERS	SUPERVISORS	ORGANIZATION RELATIONSHIPS
1	2	6
1	3	18

FIG. 10. Data showing the rapid increase in organizational relationships as the number of persons increases.

Wide spans of authority make for a high number of organizational relationships, while short spans make for a low number of relationships. Not all the relationships are of equal importance, but they should be taken into account when determining the span of authority.

RESPONSIBILITY

When a management member is given or assumes authority to perform specific work, an obligation to perform the work is created. The acceptance of this obligation is known as responsibility which can be defined as follows. *Responsibility is the obligation for the carrying out of a duty and what one is accountable for in the execution of an assigned task.* That is, responsibility can be viewed as having two parts: (1) the obligation to secure results and (2) the accountability to the one from whom the authority is received. Commonly responsibility takes the form of a list of duties. These are general statements—they do not spell out every detail of what is to be performed.

Being obligated to secure results and being accountable automatically puts a person under pressure and develops his sensitivity to gain satisfactory results. Typically, in a business enterprise the board of directors appoints a president who is expected to manage the business. His obligation to secure results and his accountability are well known. In turn, by means of organizing, he shares his authority and responsibility with individuals. In fact, this is one of the main purposes of organizing.

Efforts to develop responsibility in management members takes many different forms, but an effective practice is to provide the holder of authority and responsibility with a list of questions to improve the exercise of his authority and to stimulate his enthusiastic acceptance of his responsibility. Figure 11 illustrates the type of questions that can be asked.

---

1. Do you make a continuing review of excess office processing capacity?
2. What five office work areas require most of your time? Should they?
3. Have you investigated to find out if your instructions are understood?
4. Are you keeping up with the latest developments in office machines that might be used in your organizational unit?
5. Are written procedures brought up to date?
6. Do you receive any useless reports or documents?
7. Do you take an individual interest in each of your subordinates?

FIG. 11.   Questions to develop management responsibility.

DELEGATION OF AUTHORITY

A very important concept in organizing is delegation of authority. This is the granting or conferring of authority by one executive to another. Usually it is thought of as being from a higher to a lower level, as is commonly the case within business enterprises. However, in some organizations of government and some religious groups, delegation of authority is from a lower to a higher level and from one level to another on the same plane. Hence delegation can be downward, upward, or outward.

By means of delegation, an executive spreads his area of managerial influence and makes an organization structure meaningful. Without delegation, an executive restricts his managerial actions to those that he himself can perform. In fact, organizing does not become fully effective until delegation of authority is practiced.

Figure 12 illustrates the importance of delegation of authority in an organization. At the top of the illustration, office executive A has three assistants, 1, 2, and 3. In turn, assistant 1 has chiefs 11 and 12 reporting to him; likewise, chief 11 has subordinates 21 and 22; and chief 12, subordinates 23 and 24. The employees reporting to executives 2 and 3 are shown by the illustration. President A delegates proper authority to his executives 1, 2, and 3. The former two, 1 and 2, delegate authority to their subordinates; and in turn, these subordinates delegate authority to their subordinates. In contrast, executive 3 is trying to do all the managerial work of his organizational unit himself. He does not delegate authority to either 15 or 16, who likewise do not delegate to 29, 30, 31, or 32. This failure to delegate authority actually paralyzes this portion of the organizational structure under executive 3. To a great extent, the employees reporting to executive 3 may just as well not be management members of the organization. There is in reality no formal authority structure below executive 3.

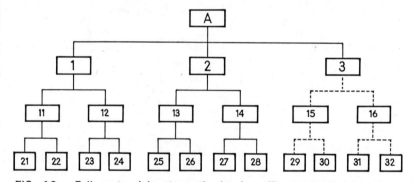

FIG. 12.   Failure to delegate authority by office executive 3 tends to paralyze the organization established under him.

In delegation, the delegator always retains his overall authority for the delegated duties. He does not surrender or permanently release his authority. He does grant the right for others to act officially within the specific areas. Only the authority needed to carry out successfully the assigned functions is or should be delegated. This makes for the tapering concept of authority and simply means that in most organization structures the authority becomes successively smaller or tapered as successively lower horizontal levels of the structure are considered.

Since an authority delegator retains in the ultimate all his authority, he likewise retains in the ultimate all his responsibility. He cannot evade a failure of a subordinate by saying it was the fault of the subordinate. The superior retains the ultimate responsibility and is accountable for what is or is not achieved by his organizational unit.

From the practical viewpoint, delegation of authority is either specially granted or inherently implied in the job. In the former case, it is given to an individual in order that he may act to perform the management which is essential in achieving the objective. In the latter case, the authority is inherently tied up with the job, so that whoever holds the job or performs the delegation function in the organization structure automatically possesses the authority which goes with that position. In any enterprise, therefore, authority is contingent upon such things as the delegation of those already in authority, the traditional structure of the organization, and the character and mental characteristics of the individual.

PROBLEM OF DELEGATION

One of the big problems in organizing is to get managers to delegate authority. Ideally, the proper delegation should exist at each delegator-to-delegatee level throughout the entire structure, and the delegation should extend as close to the level or point of action as possible. This makes for effective organizational action and encourages initiative by employees at each organization level. But in practice, some managers are reluctant to delegate. They fear that if authority is delegated, the right decision may not be made, and the work will not be handled correctly. Their belief is that they must keep in close touch with activities and decide most issues. In some instances, they may not fully realize the amount of authority needed by a subordinate to get the work done properly. In other instances, the manager states that he has delegated authority but at the same time criticizes his subordinates when they make and enforce decisions without his advice.

Delegation of authority is not easily acquired. The natural tendency is to do work yourself if you are the one charged with doing it. And if the work is important, there is all the more reason for doing it yourself to make certain that it is done right. These habits develop quite commonly because most persons acquire managerial status after doing nonmanagerial work. The latter type emphasizes doing the work yourself and doing it well; the reward can be promotion to managerial work. But success in managerial work requires getting work achieved by and through others. Failure to realize this fact plus difficulty in making the needed change in thinking, i.e., acquiring the managerial viewpoint, not the direct operative viewpoint, contribute to the lack of delegation by a manager.

It is common for the amount and extent of delegation of authority to be arrived at informally by trial and error. The subordinate makes a decision or tries out a certain practice; and if no reprimand results, he assumes the management work performed is within his province. In many cases, the status of delegation of authority is the result of an infiltration process over a long period of time. Slowly but surely, authority for certain matters has been turned over to the delegatee. Commonly, verbal statements establish the amount of delegation of authority; and in a relatively few instances, the superior gives specific delegation of authority in writing.

DEVELOPING DELEGATION OF AUTHORITY

The first requirement for developing delegation of authority is to realize the need for it. A manager must recognize that as long as he is limited to doing what he can accomplish himself, he will always be short of time and limited in his achievements. The alternative is to acquire aides, train them, and permit them to do the job, even if their manner of doing it differs from how the manager might have done it. Competent aides are mandatory for group efforts to reach greatest heights. A manager's need is to multiply himself. It is nonsense to try to lead the band and play all the instruments, too.

Furthermore, for delegation to work effectively, certain criteria can assist materially. Important is the establishment of definite goals and clear policies, for these give guidance to the subordinate and keep him from going too far astray in the fulfillment of the tasks. Work which is routine and which is covered by definite policies should offer little delegation difficulty. Clear and timely communication, complete instructions and orders, and definite job identifications are also helpful. And the use of broad controls expedites delegation, for they can supply the desired checks to determine whether the work is being accomplished satisfactorily.

Lastly, belief in delegation is necessary. An office manager must want to make delegation successful; he must strive to help it succeed. Among other things, he will not interpret delegation as distributing the work to others, sitting back, and observing if they make good or not. Rather, he will select the delegatee carefully and offer counsel readily to him, being careful not to give him answers, but to help him find the answers himself. The office manager must be willing to see his subordinates make mistakes and charge the cost to management training and the strengthening of his organization. Effective delegating does not just happen. From the very beginning, it takes much effort, time, and persistence to develop the art of authority delegation and to keep it alive.

LINE AUTHORITY AND STAFF AUTHORITY

Full comprehension of organizing also requires knowledge of the types of authority, their respective characteristics, and when to use what type for which purpose. The two main classifications of authority are (1) line and (2) staff. A manager can have either or both. When a manager has line authority, he is called a "line manager" and normally exercises direct command over the work of all members in his unit, but there are certain exceptions, as discussed below. Characteristically, the authority relationship is of a superior-subordinate type, forming "a line" from the top to the bottom of the structure. It is the authority used to accomplish directly the major goals of an enterprise and exists at all levels of the organization structure.

Staff authority, the second major classification, is made up of several different types including (1) advisory staff, (2) functional staff, (3) service staff, and (4) control staff. All of these are commonly termed "staff authority," yet they are dissimilar in important respects, and the common identification of staff is unfortunate. A manager with staff authority is a staff manager. A clear understanding of these various types of staff authority helps clarify vital relationships in organizing. All are in use and are believed necessary. Their specific application depends upon the individual organization.

ADVISORY STAFF AUTHORITY

The word "staff," according to Webster, means "a pole carried in the hand for support." Therefore, staff authority pertains to assistance or support, and this concept was the initial identification and use given staff authority. Much of this assistance and support takes the form of being advisory and is appropriately called advisory staff authority. Specifically, a manager with advisory staff authority normally counsels or advises, in his specialty, the manager having line authority. Advisory staff is a manager-to-manager relationship and can exist within any organizational level.

In Figure 13, line manager L has four subordinates, S, L_1, L_2, and L_3. The latter three are line executives, while S is an advisory staff executive. His job essentially is to counsel and advise L in his (S's) specialty so that L can do a better job. The counsel and advice of S can be

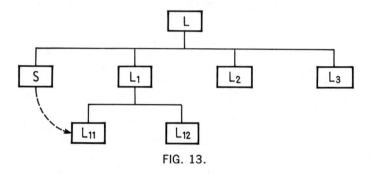

FIG. 13.

accepted in whole or part and utilized by L in managing the organizational group; or L can reject the advice of S, since L is in direct command of the unit. In some companies, the practice of "compulsory staff service" is followed. This requires a line executive to listen to his staff executives, but the final decision and enforcement rests with the line executive. When the managers are competent, this practice aids them in their respective tasks. Also, in some enterprises, the "completed staff work" doctrine is followed. This emphasizes the presentation of complete solutions by the advisory staff to the line executives. Piecemeal recommendations are avoided; and stress is placed on supplying assistance, not placing the line man in a predicament with questions regarding what he wants investigated or what data should be included in a report. Of course, the line man and the staff man should talk things over, but in a constructive way, with each making contributions.

FUNCTIONAL STAFF AUTHORITY

In office management, the use of functional staff authority is especially common. It concerns specific functions only and is delegated from one manager to another manager who is not related to the former by formally established authority channels. It can be conferred by a line to a staff manager, or vice versa. To illustrate, in Figure 13, line manager L may delegate to his subordinate staff executive, S, the authority for S to issue orders concerning a specific work activity directly to L_{11}, who is a line manager. In this case, the authority possessed by S is functional staff. Actually, L is delegating a qualified amount of line authority for a specific activity to S. The delegated authority is limited to a particular activity and applies only to the authority relationship in this activity between S and L_{11}. Good management practices would include L's informing L_1, L_{11}, and L_{12} that this functional staff authority exists. Functional staff authority expedites efficiency and is convenient. Its use, however, must necessarily be limited; otherwise, established authority relationships are neutralized. Some specialized activities of the office from time to time require a competent office executive to explain and enforce office procedures to nonoffice personnel in order to insure proper handling and good administration. Such situations are solved by the use of functional authority.

SERVICE STAFF AUTHORITY

When speaking of office organizing, the term "service unit" commonly arises. Its justification is primarily economy and improved work performed or service offered by the unit. Purchasing, general office services (mail, telephone, and reception service), and legal counsel are examples of service organizational units. Generally, the head of such a unit possesses service staff authority which actually includes some line authority, as persons are expected to request the service organization unit to perform for them a service included in the service unit's makeup and, furthermore, to be bound by the decisions made by the service unit in its specialty. To illustrate, the manager of billing may not purchase supplies and equipment. This is done for him by the purchasing unit, and the billing manager abides by the decisions and actions of the purchasing unit.

Service staff authority applies both within and outside of the service unit as it pertains to this specialized service work. In addition, some service organizational units utilize functional authority when delegated, that is, they have jurisdiction over specific work performed by others not normally or formally under the authority of the service unit. In some instances, the service unit's authority is limited to the strictly advisory. The unit recommends and counsels in work regarding its specialty, but the decision as to what to do and its enforcement are not within the province of the service unit.

CONTROL STAFF AUTHORITY

In many organizations, there are units that perform essential work for achieving the major goals of the enterprise; yet, their work is of a specialty nature and is not supplied on a strictly advisory basis. The contribution is indirect insofar as the chief objectives are concerned; but when necessary enforcement of decisions is present, considerable line authority over the particular function in the enterprise may be present. For example, these conditions frequently exist for an auditing unit, or a procedural analysis organization unit, or one dealing with office standards.

Requests by such a unit to line managers to supply certain financial information, to use financial standards supplied, and to abide by prescribed auditing practices are not on a "take it or leave it" basis by the line managers. The requests are essential for required managerial control and when they can be enforced by the auditing unit, such a unit has control staff authority. In a very real sense, it includes aspects of ultimate line authority. Enforcement is usually voluntary because the line managers realize that the specialty offered is important and that, if necessary, compliance with requests can and will be forthcoming.

ORGANIZATION CHARTS

An organization chart is a graphic representation of an organization structure. It can be thought of as a picture of the organization structure; it shows the organizational units, the relationships, and the existing lines of authority.

To draw an organization chart, use the outline approach. First, list the main functions; next, place those functions which are subordinate to the main functions under the proper main function in the outline list; then, place under each subordinate function the minor functions which properly belong under the respective subordinate function. In this way, a list is developed which shows the main functions, the subordinates under each main function, and the minor functions under each subordinate. This outline form is then transformed into the graphic form which makes up the organization chart.

The chart may also be prepared by starting with the person of highest authority in the organization structure and working down by determining who reports to this top person and what activities each person handles. This procedure provides the information for the first level of management below the chief executive and may be followed for each consecutive layer. From the information so gathered, the organization chart can be constructed.

An organization chart simply helps in visualizing the organization structure; it insures neither good organization nor good management. However, it does compel the organizer to put down in black and white what the structural relationships are. This crystallizes his thinking and clarifies fuzzy, but important, details which might otherwise be overlooked. Specifically, the main advantages of an organization chart can be listed as follows: (1) a clear, overall concept of the organization is obtained; (2) the main lines of authority and responsibility are brought out in full relief; (3) promotional possibilities are provided; and (4) the assignment of titles is simplified.

THE LINE ORGANIZATION

The line, or scalar, type of organization, which was used extensively in our early industrial development, is one of the oldest organization forms. It uses line authority exclusively. This type of organization is still quite popular and is frequently employed by proprietors of small businesses and for other enterprises where the number of employees is small.

The line organization is characterized by direct lines of authority from the top executive to the various assistants, and direct from them to the employees at the operative level. Each member is fully responsible for the carrying out or the actual performance of the job to be done. Throughout the entire structure, each member is in complete charge of all activities within his particular organization segment. Authority and responsibility are greatest at the top, and reduce or taper as successively lower levels of management are considered.

The line type of organization is illustrated in Figure 14. Line authority exists between the president at the top and the employees at the bottom. The line authority may be thought of as a scalar type, in that it reduces by scales or steps. To illustrate, the connection is from the president to the vice-president of finance, to the manager in charge of office work, to the supervisor of the mail, telephone, and reception services section, and to the clerks of this section. The vice-president of finance is in complete charge of finance, including the work of the manager in charge of office work and the manager in charge of credits, disbursements, and equities of the company; the manager in charge of office work is, in turn, in complete charge of that particular segment of the organization and specifically over the supervisors of correspondence and filing; records, procedures, and manuals; and mail, telephone, and reception services.

The advantages of the line organization include the following: Authority and responsibility are definitely fixed, and the person who has that authority and responsibility is known to all; the structure is very simple and hence readily understood by all personnel; discipline is easily maintained, since each worker and each boss knows what is expected of him and in which areas he is to operate; decisions can be quickly reached; the fact that a single boss who is in complete charge makes for a minimum of delay in decision reaching; and lastly, the line organization offers splendid training opportunities for the development of executive talent. The line officer is charged with getting things executed; he must be a doer; he must get the work accomplished.

In contrast, the line organization also has its disadvantages. Perhaps most outstanding is that, relatively, specialization of work is not

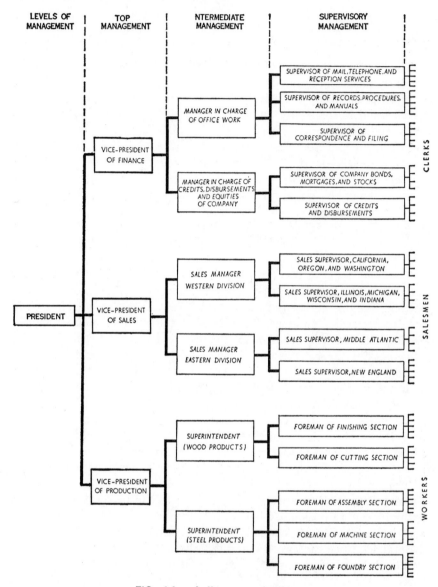

FIG. 14.   A line organization.

practiced. Particularly is this true at the intermediate and supervisory management levels. Another disadvantage is the difficulty of securing coordination. Each lord is master of his own house or his unit of the organization, and the coordination between any two line units of the same organizational level is obtained solely by the strong leadership of the man at the top in charge of the several line units. The tendency is for the head of each unit to develop a rather independent unit and to think only of his own unit's activities, without much regard for other necessary functions of the enterprise. In fact, some believe that the line organization probably places too much emphasis on the managers. Another disadvantage is the difficulty of forming organizational units; this is particularly true in cases where the unit is not suggested by the process. Frequently, insufficient opportunity is afforded to modify and to change existing units from the viewpoint of the total organization structure.

THE LINE AND STAFF ORGANIZATION

When staff authority relationships are added to a line organization, the resultant organization is called a line and staff organization which is extensively used. In this type, line managers have line authority to carry out the activities, but their efforts are qualified by staff managers who have authority to carry out their particular work. Both line and staff managers are considered essential, and all are believed needed to accomplish the work effectively. More precisely this means that the line and the staff managers comprise a winning team of managers with varying degrees and types of authority. In the team effort, all are required. None should be thought of as inferior; for if in fact they are, then either they should be replaced or their area of operation should be eliminated.

The chart of a line and staff organization is shown in Figure 15. The line part of this organization, basically the same as that shown in Figure 14–2 is represented by the diagram *outside* the areas of the dotted circles, and the areas *inside* the six circles represent staff organizational functions. On the left, under production, for example, the jobs of plant manager, chief inspector, and methods and standards manager constitute staff activities. Likewise, under the vice-president in charge of sales, the jobs of market development and sales and market research constitute staff functions. The entire portion of the chart to the right, under personnel, is circled, since personnel is a staff function to the entire organization. Areas enclosed by circles 2 and 3 represent staff functions at lower levels of management. Staff functions can exist at all levels. Note in particular that even though a function is staff, the organization for carrying out that function may be of a line organization type. To illustrate, under the vice-president of sales, the directorship of the sales and market research division is a staff activity to the organization structure as a whole; but the sales and market research division itself is organized as a line organization, with the work of market potentials and consumer opinions under it.

The advantages of the line and staff organization are many. First, the

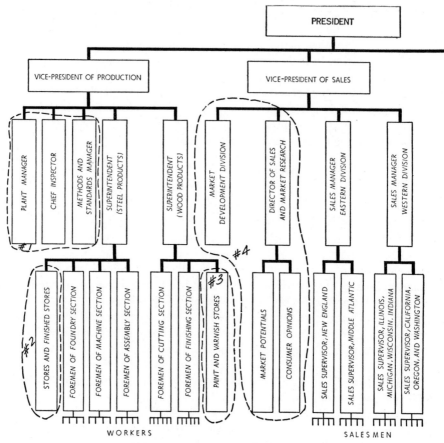

FIG. 15. A line and staff organization.

lines of authority are fairly well fixed, good discipline can be attained, decisions can be reached after desirable deliberation, and the principle of specialization can be utilized to the extent of practical limits. Second, coordination can be improved because the line officers are supplied with factual data concerning activities both within and outside their own units. Third, flexibility is provided for the organization structure to expand or contract, as conditions warrant. New activities can be added and old ones discarded without seriously affecting the organization structure. Fourth, proper balance among all the activities, line as well as staff, can be maintained. Fifth, more opportunities are afforded to match the desires, capacities, and interests of personnel with the job, since a greater variety of jobs involving different duties, responsibilities, training, and background is required.

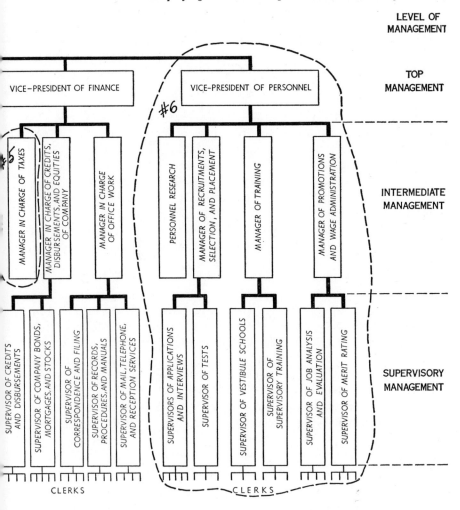

The disadvantages of the line and staff organization center around the relationships existing between the line and staff managers. In the first place, the line manager may tend to ignore the advisory staff manager's counsel, so that the expert information provided is never used. Second, the staff manager may tend to ignore the ideas of the line manager simply because specialization and expertness are supposed to be under the jurisdiction of the staff manager. Third, the staff manager may overstep his prescribed staff authority and even attempt to take over line authority which is out of his realm of activity. Fourth, a considerable number of staff managers are not good salesmen, and many staff contributions are not fully used partly because other managers are not convinced of the merits of the staff's work. Fifth, line orders, staff advice, and staff orders may be confused by members of the organization structure, with the result that the *what, when, where,* and *how* of activities are not clearly known to either the managers or the nonmanagement members.

USE OF COMMITTEES

Committees constitute an important part of most organization structures. They can exist at any organizational level, be of short or of long life, and deal with various subjects. Many are delegated line authority, that is, they not only discuss and decide issues but also secure compliance of others with the decision. Such a committee is sometimes called a "plural executive." However, probably most committees have advisory staff authority. Their purpose is to discuss and recommend. In some cases, they simply receive information, classify it, and make it available for others to use.

The committee may be viewed as an important modification or addition to the main type of organization. Just as staff modifies the line to form a line and staff organization, so the committee may also be added to form a line, staff, and committee organization. In this case, the committee element adds an excellent medium to the organizational structure for discussion and educational group meetings. Also, the committee acting in an advisory capacity serves as an excellent addition.

A committee offers several outstanding advantages. First, it permits organization members to take an active part; thus, better cooperation is obtained. Second, it helps to secure coordination. Men and women from different departments have the chance to see the organization's needs as a whole; they have a chance to discuss these problems with their fellow supervisors and employees. Third, the committee is an excellent source of collective advice, ideas, and opinions for top managers. Fourth, the committee offers an excellent medium for educational and training purposes.

In contrast, a disadvantage of the use of a committee is that it divides responsibility. There is no single individual fully responsible. Second, the committee is weak in carrying out activities. It commonly lacks decisive action and follow-up. Third, most of a committee's decisions are the result of compromise—a "straddle the fence" variety. Usually, the majority rules; and this might tend to bring prejudice, secret agreements, and bargaining, rather than facts only, into the committee's decisions. Fourth, committee meetings usually require a great deal of the members' time. There appears to be little doubt that a sizable amount of this time is wasted and might better be spent by members on their individual tasks.

CHAPTER FOUR

OFFICE SUPERVISING

*The secret of good direction does not consist
in solving problems but in identifying them.*
—*L. A. Appley*

SUPERVISORS are key personnel in an office organization. Every office organization unit is what it is largely because of the supervisor's influence. Actually, many problems are reduced to simple tasks when supervisors are competent, receive cooperation from their subordinates, and utilize effective organization. The accomplishment of satisfactory office production and the establishment of a favorable work climate depend in large measure upon the quality of office supervision. The supervisor is charged with seeing that the work in his unit is performed within a reasonable time and at a reasonable cost. He is the ultimate regulator of what is accomplished.

In addition, and equally as important, supervisors are responsible for a great deal of the managerial actuating that is done. As stated in Chapter 1, actuating commonly stresses the concept of the individual, not that of a group. In other words, actuating in management is most frequently applied to an individual human being and the type of actuation is both carefully selected and applied in keeping with the particular characteristics of the individual. Since plans, policies, and decisions originated by top managers must filter down through the various levels of management, supervisors are in a strategic location, and they exercise significant influence in the selection and the implementation of the various actuating techniques.

MANAGERIAL ACTUATING

A definition of managerial actuating is in order. It is *the creating and the continuing of the desire by each member of an enterprise to achieve work goals willingly and enthusiastically.* From a manager's viewpoint, actuating can be thought of as the ability to get others to do the work the manager wants done because they want to do it. To many, actuating is of foremost importance in the management of office work. There is no question that high managerial efficiency is attainable when office personnel are inspired, have great desire, and are called upon to use their highest attainable skills and capacities in work they are genuinely interested in doing.

THE SUPERVISOR'S STATUS

The supervisor is at the critical focal point about which his superiors' wishes and instructions are distributed, and his subordinates' desires are concentrated. The supervisor is the point of contact between a high and the next succeeding lower level of management members and between management members at the lowest management level and nonmanagement members. For any group the supervisor represents the higher level of management for that group or the management member for a group of nonmanagement members. The terms, middle manager, intermediate manager, operative manager, and the like are sometimes used; but they all denote a person engaged in supervisory work, or more specifically, they all perform managerial actuating efforts.

However, quite commonly a supervisor is thought of as being below what might be termed the executive level. A supervisor's work is similar to that of the executive; but the scope of the work, the matters on which decisions must be made, and the general overall executive work are not as broad in the case of the supervisor as in the case of the executive. For convenience and going along with what is the most popular version, "supervisor" can be defined as a *management member working at an organizational level where personal oversight of tasks assigned to small groups is usually assumed in order to assure satisfactory performance.*

THE WORK OF THE SUPERVISOR

Actually the supervisor's work, in great measure, consists of getting work performed properly by others. This is the heart of supervisory success. A person who insists upon doing everything himself never makes a satisfactory supervisor. Most failures in supervision are in getting things done through people. It is not always the employee's fault, although this is the common explanation.

It is possible to classify the work of the supervisor in a variety of ways. Since the supervisor is a management member, the following outline appears logical and helpful.

Under planning, the supervisor has such activities as:

1. Participating in the formulation of establishing objectiv/ unit.
2. Understanding and knowing the work to be done.
3. Knowing and interpreting company policies to the employee.
4. Keeping up with new developments.
5. Improving current methods being followed.

Regulating encompasses the following work by the supervisor:

1. Following stated practices and procedures.
2. Utilizing standards established for the work.
3. Evaluating work output in terms of cost.
4. Checking accuracy and quantity of work.
5. Minimizing peak work loads.

Organizing efforts by the supervisor include:

1. Delegating work to others.
2. Allocating the work among members of the unit.
3. Placing similar work in the same unit.
4. Establishing proper authority relationships among members of a unit.
5. Keeping employee-work relationships up to date.

The supervisor's managerial actuating efforts deal with:

1. Informing employees of changes.
2. Evaluating and disciplining employees.
3. Developing understudies.
4. Securing teamwork and harmony among employees.
5. Increasing the value of employees.

KNOWLEDGE AND SKILL OF THE SUPERVISOR

To perform his work effectively, the supervisor must have certain knowledge and must be able to do skillfully certain activities. Knowledge requirements of the supervisor vary from one office to another, but the ability to perform certain activities skillfully is fairly constant regardless of the office and its type of work.

The basic knowledge needs are:

1. *Technical knowledge.* This includes knowledge of systems, procedures, materials, office forms, equipment, and the manner in which results

are used. Much of this knowledge might be acquired while one is serving in a nonsupervisory capacity. The supervisor should know enough about the detail work that is done to provide the necessary leadership to those performing the tasks and to plan and control their work so that orderly and reasonable rates of accomplishment are realized.

2. *Knowledge of responsibilities.* This includes comprehension of the company's policies, rules, and regulations; of the extent of the supervisor's authority and responsibility; and of matters on which he can make final decisions. An acquaintance with basic information about organization, management, collective bargaining, communication, budgeting, and any area of direct or indirect concern in the particular supervisory job appears to be a minimum requirement.

Basic needs concerning what the supervisor's skills are:

1. *Skill in teaching.* Whether a supervisor gives specific instructions on a particular task or makes assignments in fairly broad terms, it is necessary that he pass along his knowledge to others and develop them. This, in turn, calls for skill in teaching and is a prime means for making supervision more effective. Generally, an employee is more satisfied, has greater interest, and will be more industrious when informed clearly what work is wanted and how it is to be performed. This means that the supervisor should have skill in instructing, so that a well-trained work force is available.

2. *Skill in methods improvement*. Better utilization of materials, machines, and manpower is the constant aim of progressive managers. Some methods of performing work are inherited, others are hastily thrown together, while still others are copied from similar operations. All can be improved. Skill in analyzing, supplemented by ingenuity, usually results in improved ways of performing work.

3. *Skill in human relations.* This sometimes suffers as a result of the pressure and volume of day-to-day work. Working with and getting along with people are vital to the supervisor. This emphasizes the important areas of understanding the behavior and attitudes of individual employees and of recognizing and using basic human motivations.

RELATIONSHIPS WITH OTHERS IN ORGANIZATION

The destiny of a supervisor is controlled largely by other people. Almost everything he achieves comes as a result of their approval. Good relationships with others in the organization are therefore paramount for the supervisor. It is the supervisor who provides the intended meaning to organizational relationships. He is the one who coordinates at his point of operation all the decisions made by those with staff authority to those with line authority. And he is the one who tempers the planned means of performing work to the actual realities of work performance at the point of their performance. For convenience we can view the supervisor's relationships as those dealing with organization members (1) above the supervisor and (2) below the supervisor.

With reference to the first, the supervisor is expected to implement a specific portion of a plan at the operative level. To do this, he is given instructions, receives specialized assistance from various staff members, attends indoctrination meetings, and communicates with his superiors. In these relationships, the astute supervisor discovers that certain practices assist him appreciably. He should:

1. *Have firm belief in essentiality of supervisory work.* The effective office supervisor believes that the office is a vital part of the enterprise and that his efforts to help manage the office work are fundamental to the success of the enterprise. He should reveal this belief by viewing enthusiastically his opportunity to contribute to the success of the office.

2. *Focus appeals to superior's greatest interests.* Normally these are improved service, lower costs of operation, and increased net income. The office supervisor who shows how his unit will help achieve these goals will capture the attention and support of his superiors. Actually, with some concentrated thinking, it is not difficult to do this, but some showmanship should be used in presenting the idea. For example, for a project lowering the costs of operation, the mere statement, "The savings to be realized are $12,000," is not nearly as effective as "The savings to be realized are greater than the net income realized from increasing our sales $125,000." Both statements mean the same thing, but the second one is far more effective to top-level managers.

3. *Expect some resistance to suggestions and new ideas.* Some top and middle managers favor a sort of "do not disturb things, let them be as they are" attitude. Especially is this true if there are no complaints and things are running quite smoothly. The feeling is: "Why take a chance? Let well enough alone." The possibility of this condition's existing in any particular case should be realized and taken into account by the office supervisor.

4. *Act in a manner to justify recognition as a member of management.* Too frequently, recognition of supervisors as management members is lip service only, the recognition is by decree only. Nothing tangible is done to make supervisors a part of management or to make them feel that they are. To overcome this condition, supervisors can offer, as a group,

suggested measures to their superiors to give them proper recognition and justify them (the supervisors) as the best means for obtaining certain goals of top management and for the overall improvement of the total management team. Top priority should be given the adopting of written statements outlining the supervisor's authority and responsibility, adequate compensation, and direct two-way flow of management information. These activities, along with other important ones and the tools for achieving them, are shown in graphic form in Figure 16.

With reference to the second category of relationships—those with organization members below the supervisor—a number of considerations can be stated. Much of the success of a supervisor depends upon his ability to develop and maintain good relationships with his work group because, as a manager, he accomplishes the work by means of this group's efforts. The supervisor is expected to utilize his employees' capacities and interests effectively. He assigns employees definite work, points out certain goals, and gets them to want to perform accurately and do a satisfactory volume of work. In addition, he is called upon to review and evaluate the work performance of his employees, and to answer questions concerning the methods in action to accomplish the work. Various means can be used by the supervisor, depending mainly upon the type of employee, the work situation, and the kind of office work.

A supervisor's relationships with members of his group emphasize use of motivating and human relations practices. To avoid repetition, we will briefly outline the following five guides that a supervisor should follow:

1. *Judge members of his group by their good qualities.* Work is achieved by positive attitudes, not by stressing lack of abilities and skills.

2. *Make every personal contact helpful and constructive.* Take the viewpoint that you are trying to assist every member of your group achieve the ultimate of his potential.

3. *Get your group members to participate in your plans.* Modify plans to strengthen them and to uncover and eliminate objections; and adopt the plan that will achieve the predetermined goal most effectively and serve the interests and desires of the group to a maximum.

4. *Eliminate opposition of interests among your group.* Find out common motives and areas of identical purpose. These should be emphasized in supervisory work. Strive toward group unity and effective teamwork.

5. *Give instructions clearly.* Be certain the basic idea is identified and transferred to the recipient of the instruction. Do not take anything for granted. Provide sufficient details.

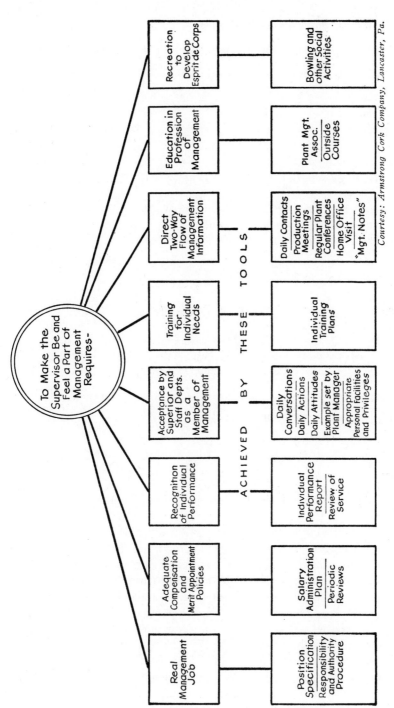

FIG. 16.   The supervisor in management.

Figure 17 shows a daily check list for a supervisor to appraise himself in his relationships with his work group.

	Yes	*No*
1. Do I impress people as knowing my job?	_____	_____
2. Do I plan my work so that each member of my group is fully occupied?	_____	_____
3. Do I follow the rules that I require of my members?	_____	_____
4. Do I have time to talk over with my members problems that are bothering them?	_____	_____
5. Do I have control of myself before I discipline any member of my group?	_____	_____
6. Do I maintain recognized quality standards?	_____	_____
7. Do I insist that each member meet reasonable work outputs?	_____	_____
8. Do I see that each member keeps his working place in an orderly condition?	_____	_____
9. Do I make certain that satisfactory working conditions are maintained?	_____	_____
10. Do I treat each member of my group as I would like to be treated?	_____	_____

FIG. 17.   Daily check list for supervisor's self-appraisal.

COACHING AND COUNSELING

The office supervisor has frequent occasion to make use of coaching and counseling. Coaching stresses the values of information and inspiration. The particular data needed for a given situation are supplied and the unique capacities of members of a group are both stimulated and integrated by a coach. In contrast, counseling emphasizes leading a person to self-insight and improvement by means of carefully selected questions and suggestions along with skillful listening. To get the person to see what he can do to improve his accomplishments is the goal of counseling. It can be viewed as a suggestive and supportive technique to instill self-motivation in the person being counseled.

To be able to use coaching and counseling successfully it is first necessary to make clear what you want the employee to do and to be sure that he knows it too. This supplies the needed orientation and something toward which he can measure his progress. Second, be sensitive to capabilities, behavior, and likes of the employee. Some excel in physical pursuits, others rank high in mental endeavors. Some are "detailists," others comprehend mainly broad generalities. Find out these individual differences and be guided by them in coaching and counseling. In brief, know your employee. Next, stress the immediate future. Concentrate on the present job. Reach agreement on what is to be done for the next day, next week, or next month at most. It is easy to make commitments for three or four years ahead and then gradually forget about them. Fourth, stay with specific, concrete examples. Talk about actual happenings. Discuss actual incidents and their effect upon his work and standing. Lastly, use constructive criticism. Tie in with his work and bring out ways which would make for improvement. Stress the potential gains and the feasibility of his achieving them.

SUPERVISING FEMALE EMPLOYEES

Since the majority of office employees are female, the subject of supervising female employees is important. In many respects, what has been stated about supervision applies equally to female and to male employees. Certain additional suggestions, however, may prove beneficial. A cardinal point is to give very careful consideration to women's work assignments. They do many things extremely well, but usually are outstanding on work requiring manual dexterity, caring, and mediating functions. That is, women are more likely to do better in work where patience, interest in human beings, and human needs are considerations. But women, like men, should be encouraged to do what they can do or what they can learn to do. It is also helpful to treat each female employee as an individual. Many women feel that their problems are different— even though other women have the same problems. Let them stand as individuals, in fact, encourage this viewpoint which usually meets with favorable response.

Pay correspondingly greater attention to the workplace of women employees. Women want "a nice place to work," including a clean, attractive area with good decor. They are actively aware of their surroundings. An opportunity for socializing, conversing with others, and allowance for family obligations are also desirable. Furthermore, exercise authority, but don't be a tyrant. Women office employees expect authority to be used and they won't rebel against it. What they won't tolerate is tyranny. Finally, recognize certain facts about the psychology of women. They tend *to show* their emotions more readily than men, probably because it is more culturally acceptable in our society. Moods in women differ and change throughout the day. With ten women employees there can be ten different moods at one time. These moods vary or multiply during the day. Frequently, female supervisors are more rigid than male supervisors would be. This is because there is a tendency for women supervisors to act as they think men would act under the same situation. The answer here is to point out that the best supervisor is both firm and considerate. Fairness must be a part of all supervisory efforts. Also recognize that all supervisors must earn the respect and confidence of his or her subordinates. It is inevitable that the work group test the new supervisor.

THE SUPERVISOR AND PLANNING

Effective supervision requires thorough planning. The successful supervisor has found that planning enables him to gain his goal with a minimum of effort. Planning helps the supervisor to maintain the proper balance in his work; major objectives are given the major portion of his time and effort. Also, planning makes for orderliness in supervision; actions are thought through. Likewise, areas of nonaction are predetermined. The supervisor knows what he is going to do and when he is going to do it.

Failure of the supervisor to plan his work results in inefficiencies and makes the job of supervision more difficult. Frequently, the lack of planning results in a failure to meet expectancies or to anticipate and to prevent supervisory problems before they occur. Other indications of lack of planning are tardiness in getting work accomplished, excessive costs, not enough time to finish the work, low morale, lack of direction to the group, waste of material, loss of employees' time, and an absence of overall coordinated effort.

Adequate planning will help disclose to the supervisor the proper time for the presentation of an idea or program to his superiors or to his subordinates. Logically, this is when they are in a receptive mood or are puzzled with a problem for which the idea or program is a solution. Timing, however, is very important; and in many cases, it is wise to draw up an entire plan, *file it away,* and let it stay filed away until the most opportune time arrives.

When this time arrives, the best technique is to submit the plan, request approval or acceptance, and give reasons why it should be followed. This approach gives the initiative to the supervisor, and the advantage commonly lies with the one having the initiative. An army with unrivaled offensive power is usually the victor; a football team with a terrific offense is extremely difficult to defeat. Games are usually not won by the team which cannot score; the best they can hope for is a tie score, or a "break" which brings them an unexpected victory.

EFFECTIVE TIME-USE BY THE SUPERVISOR

Basic to supervisory success is the wise use of time on the job. To this end, the office supervisor can concentrate on essentials—the really important tasks. The best supervisors perform key tasks only and do not let themselves get involved in endless details. Unnecessary work is quickly identified as such and abolished. Also, for most supervisors, the completion of a task once it is started makes for efficient time utilization. Tasks not quite finished are the vexation of many supervisors. Staying with a job until it is finished and not giving in to interruptions are key habits to be followed. In addition, the budgeting of one's time is a time-saver. The time-minded supervisor decides what tasks he had to perform, estimates the time for each, and schedules these time periods through his workday. This approach helps utilize time more effectively and establishes goals that are achieved during the day, thus providing a sense of satisfaction. Furthermore, the office supervisor should acquire speed in reading and become more selective in what is read. Few adults receive reading training beyond the elementary school level. Many people read at this pace, which is a serious detriment to their efficiency in time utilization. By practice and accelerated reading courses increases up to 75 percent in reading efficiency can be attained.

With better utilization of time, a proper balance among the various facets of the supervisory work should be attained. An equitable appraisal of all the various supervisory tasks must be made and compared with established levels of satisfactory performance. For example, data on cost, quantity of work achieved, quality of work, number of grievances, number tardy, number absent, and labor turnover rates are helpful. Trends in these data are significant. Also, changes in some factors may help predict future changes in others—frequently before either the difficulty or the favorable accomplishment is revealed by standard operating reports.

AUTHORITY AND SELECTION OF OFFICE SUPERVISORS

In a relatively small enterprise, the general manager, who in many cases is also the owner, has supervisory authority over each employee. The general manager makes the decisions that concern job requirements, keeps the employee informed about changes and the progress of the business. With growth of the company and the resultant spreading of the gap between top management and nonmanagement members, it is generally agreed that supervisors must narrow the gap and conduct many of the needed managerial relations with employees.

The size and complexity of the enterprise, as well as the viewpoint toward employees, tend to modify the supervisor's authority. Unfortunately, in many offices, it is not clear what the office supervisor is expected to do. The former concept of the supervisor "running his unit," with complete authority to hire, fire, change work sequence, make improvements, and handle operations in any way believed satisfactory, has changed considerably in many offices. This lack of a clear-cut understanding is due to the very nature of the job—the fact that the work of supervision is so varied, the scope so large, and the activities involved so numerous. However, the transition can be said to have been brought about by the use of staff members to assist and to render advice to the supervisor in carrying out his work. In some cases, it is believed that the work of office supervising has become so complex that expert help to the supervisor is an absolute necessity. In contrast, others are of the opinion that staff helpers usurp authority and take over activities which constitute the fundamental duties of the supervisor. For example, in many offices, the supervisor does not interview and select new employees, but he does have a voice in the final hiring.

Selection of office supervisors can be considered the beginning of effective supervision. From what has already been stated, it follows that a supervisor's qualifications are different from those of an operative employee. The employee having the longest service, the highest production volume, or the longest no-tardiness and no-absenteeism record is not necessarily the best selection for a supervisory job. Much of the work the supervisor is called upon to perform differs from that of the operative employee.

The first step in the selection of office supervision is to determine the background and characteristics needed for the supervisory jobs. Such information can be used to set the minimum employment qualifications and standards. Preparation of such information should take into account the realities of the specific condition.

The actual task of selection is assisted by the use of any one or all of the following: (1) appraisals of the candidates, (2) written tests, (3) interviews, and (4) evaluation of experience and training. The first, or appraisal of candidates, can take many different forms, including inquiry of the candidate's present superior, talking with those acquainted with the candidate's work performance, and discussing with friends the candidate's activities in clubs and other groups outside the office.

Written tests are increasing in usage, but they probably do not yet qualify as a common means for office supervisory selection. Tests are designed to measure work, personality, and technical factors. They provide a means to screen initially a large number of candidates, and they stress objective evidence instead of someone's opinion and judgment. However, considerable criticism has been leveled against tests in which it is pointed out that they concentrate on selected areas rather than the "entire man," that some candidates are practically certain not to reveal their true ability by written word, and that the candidates answer test questions for a prescribed situation in one way, yet for the same situation perform in a different way under actual working conditions.

As pointed out in Chapter 9, interviewing is perhaps the most common means of selection, and this statement includes supervisory selection. The face-to-face meeting, the opportunity to clarify ambiguous written statements, and the flexibility to shape the interview to the individual case make for the wide use and popularity of the interview method.

Finally, the evaluation of experience and training provides a practical element to the selection method followed. A detailed investigation of the candidate's work history is sometimes undertaken. Thus, elements which might be overlooked in the other selection approaches are brought into the program. Knowledge of the enterprise and technical competence are illustrative of these elements.

SUPERVISORY TRAINING

Strictly speaking, any educational activity designed to prepare the candidate for supervisory work or to improve the supervisor in carrying out his duties successfully can be termed "supervisory training." The field is quite broad and deals with many, yet related, subjects. Supervisory training is not confined to learning to perform a set of movements more efficiently but includes the development of attitudes, control of emotions, and the broadening of one's views. Keeping the supervisor fully informed constitutes one of the biggest challenges in supervisory training. Conditions are constantly changing; new developments are taking place; and in most cases, the supervisor finds himself confronted with new personnel, new attitudes, and new problems.

Excellent work in supervisory training is being accomplished by the members of the Training Within Industry Foundation, a nonprofit organization which advocates gaining maximum results from employed people through better supervision. Years of intensive research and many office tryouts with groups of supervisors have helped develop highly successful training programs for supervisors. Among the more important for normal office use are:

1. *Job instruction.* The *JI* course consists of five two-hour sessions and is intended to give skill in instructing. It is especially helpful where there is work involving long break-in periods, numerous errors, or difficulty in getting the office work out on time. To illustrate the content, the course consists of four main parts: (*a*) preparing the employee, (*b*) presenting the operation, (*c*) trying out the performance, and (*d*) following up on performance.

2. *Job relations.* Known as the *JR* course, this also consists of five two-hour sessions. It helps provide skill in leadership and is recommended where there are too many misunderstandings among employees and complaints are numerous in the human relations area.

3. *Job methods.* This *JM* program likewise is five two-hour sessions. It gives skill in improving methods through practice sessions and on-the-job coaching. This program is effective in finding better methods of accomplishing office work.

4. *Job economics training.* Known as the *JET* course, this requires five $1\frac{1}{2}$-hour sessions and presents the basic principles upon which the United States economy operates.

5. *Discussion leading.* This *DL* course of four three-hour sessions is designed to give skill in getting participation in meetings and in discussing thoroughly matters of common interest.

6. *Program development.* The *PD* course is intended for the instruction of one person in a company who has responsibility for designing and conducting training programs in his company or some unit thereof. The normal time required for this course is five days, dispersed among two or three weeks, to permit specific application of program material to the trainee's company.

In addition, the following means of supervisory training are helpful and widely used:

1. *Company supervisory schools* in which organized classes in problems of supervision are studied.

2. *Individual study* of the various available materials on the theory and practice of supervisory work.

3. *Conferences and seminars* that afford discussions with supervisors of other departments, group training, and an opportunity to talk over problems of mutual interest.

4. *Dramatized meetings* in which supervisors act out their problems, this acting-out to be followed by discussions and comments to bring out possible improvements in the handling of problems.

5. *Observation of and talks with employees* to gain a better insight into their jobs and their attitudes.

6. *Interviews with top management members* to gain advice and suggestions regarding what supervisory action might be taken under various circumstances.

7. *Involvement in an actual situation,* handling the work of supervision with a "learn by doing" technique. Uusually, some background data are desirable before using this means of obtaining information.

SECURING EFFECTIVE SUPERVISION

Much material is available concerning how to be an efficient supervisor. Some of it is quite idealistic and contains many platitudes. The subject is broad, but the following ten points are included in order to indicate, in general, the type of activity which is recommended.

1. *Treat all workers alike—show no favoritism.* The successful supervisor operates objectively; his personal likes and dislikes are not permitted to influence his work.

2. *Practice consultative supervision.* This practice includes talking things over with the employees and giving them an opportunity to suggest the best way to accomplish a task. Such a procedure makes for a cooperative work force and recognizes the fact that no one has a monopoly on good ideas.

3. *Enforce all rules and regulations promptly.* Usually, nothing is gained by delaying action in cases where violations are involved. In fact, delay might be interpreted as a lack of decisiveness and an inability to cope with the situation.

4. *Keep your instructions simple, and repeat them frequently to the new employee.* Good supervision requires mutual understanding between the supervisor and the employee. In addition, a patient, helpful attitude must be assumed, particularly in working with the employee who is not yet fully familiar with all the job requirements.

5. *Insist upon and stress the need for each employee to give a full day's work for a full day's pay.* Satisfactory work outputs are the chief responsibility of every supervisor.

6. *Watch waste—material loss and time loss.* One of the chief foes of efficiency is waste. Guarding against this enemy will add significantly to the work output.

7. *Keep fully informed on company policies and their interpretation.* The supervisor is constantly called upon to interpret company policies to the employees. Knowing the policies and keeping informed of any changes and additions is a supervisory "must."

8. *Secure employees' opinions regarding supervision.* Through some means, such at attitude surveys, spot interviews, casual conversations, and

discussion groups, find out what is bothering the employees and what "gripes" are developing. Adequate and correct information at the right time and place may avoid much needless trouble.

9. *Develop capable assistants.* Good management requires that qualified replacements be available to maintain the supervisory force at a satisfactory number and caliber. Failure to develop an understudy jeopardizes the supervisor's chances for promotion.

10. *Let top and middle management members know what you are doing and why.* Because supervision is vital to the enterprise, top and middle management members should know what supervisory action is taking place. Effective supervision requires complete backing by these members, and one of the best ways to retain this endorsement is to tell them what is going on, along with the various reasons why.

CHAPTER FIVE

MOTIVATING OFFICE PERSONNEL

*You will never stub your toe standing still. The faster you go,
the more chance there is of stubbing your toe, but the
more chance you have of getting somewhere.*
                                    —Charles F. Kettering

THE true meaning, scope, significance, and importance of managerial actuating warrant full discussion. It has already been indicated that the supervisor is a key figure in the practice of actuating and in the last chapter various of his activities conditioned by actuating were described. At this point and to continue, it is helpful to relate the background, developments, and some common specific activities in management that exemplify actuating in action.

Most employees want and will respond favorably to help. They want to develop, to perform greater service, to acquire status, and to contribute importantly. This means that in many respects a manager is really a helper of employees. His task is to help his followers do their best. His challenge is to get employees to do more for him than they will for others. This means that knowledge of people's behavior and skill in influencing them are extremely important attributes of the manager. We are not concerned directly with the achievement of one big happy family of employees as such, but toward the achievement of a contented group as an essential in accomplishing the task to be performed. We manage to get work accomplished effectively, but we can do this and at the same time make the employee's work life happier and his work more meaningful and satisfying.

HISTORICAL DEVELOPMENTS OF VIEWPOINTS TOWARD EMPLOYEES

Our viewpoint toward employees was not always as it exists today. Actually, we have progressed through several stages. At one time, an employee was considered in the same light as a commodity—something to be bought on the open market, and of a fairly uniform quality. Later, the so-called machinery conception of labor became prominent; the employee was considered a producing unit and his value measured in terms of the goods produced. After years of struggle and unhappiness, a new concept of employer-employee relationships gradually evolved. It was that an employee is a human being and that his welfare is important; hence, the employer should encourage and supply various welfare services deemed desirable. A paternal attitude toward the employee developed. This represented an improvement over the employee's previous status, but it was not the answer to satisfactory employer-employee relations. Many employees were suspicious of these welfare efforts and resented being the children of a paternalistic policy. Since the period of around 1915–20, the concept that an employee is a human entity and must be treated as such has gained headway. This means that consideration for an employee's psychological makeup and recognition and utilization of his desires, attitudes, interests, and motives are as important as attention to his physical efforts, perhaps even more so.

As thinking along this human-entity line progressed, the basis for a great many current practices developed, including the idea that individuals vary in their personal aptitudes and interests, that no two people respond identically to the same opportunity, that different jobs require different abilities, that the emotional makeup of the employee is important, and that the prevailing spirit or feeling of the work force affects its productivity. A "mutuality of interests" between employer and employee is being recognized. This means that both have an interest in the well-being of the enterprise and that the relationship between employer and employee should be a harmonious working together toward their common objectives, which are compatible over the long-run period of time.

MOTIVATING EMPLOYEES

The question can be asked: "How do you motivate employees?" A logical approach is to find out the wants of the employees and either satisfy these wants in managerial activities or supply reasonable explanations why they cannot be fulfilled. Many studies have been conducted to discover the important wants of employees. The survival or biological needs, sometimes referred to as economic, include the desire for adequate food, clothing, and shelter. What constitutes adequacy in these areas will differ among people, and likewise the degree of motivations to acquire satisfaction of these needs will vary. However, in normal economic times, these survival needs are met; and when they are taken care of, much of the employee's concern is then turned to the satisfaction of emotional and social needs. For example, he wants to know that what he is doing is worthwhile and has merit, that he is accepted and approved by his fellow men. For most employees, their daily work is expected, at least in part, to supply these needs by providing an opportunity to demonstrate their talent, acquire prestige, and gain recognition.

Studies along this line reveal listings of the psychological and social wants of employees. The wants vary somewhat depending upon the study, but most include the following: job security, opportunity for expression, chance to develop and grow, information about changes that will affect them, equitable pay, personal help when requested, recognition for accomplishments, treatment as human beings, and effective supervision.

Knowing these wants, the next step is to set operations in action in order to satisfy them. Here is where the real skill of motivating enters. Employees' wants are not identical for each group or for each member of a group. Furthermore, the wants do not remain constant; they vary from day to day. And the reaction to the same stimuli may differ widely among employees.

Most people want to do their share—and more. It is the task of the manager to provide a working climate in which this basic desire of an employee is completely fulfilled. From time to time, a person is encountered who wants to "get by" without doing any work, dislikes most fellow employees, has little ethics in his dealings with others, and is against most proposals by people with whom he is associated. Such a person is sick emotionally and mentally. Study shows that in many instances, this is not the way he would like to be; but he got this way owing to his past experiences, his beliefs, or the conditions to which he was exposed. Quite frequently, it is found that this type of person actually wants help. Proper understanding and motivating can straighten him out, but it may take much time and patience.

MOTIVATION BASIS

The most successful motivation is self-direction by the employee. The urge or desire should come from within the individual, not from someone else in the form of an outside force. Hence, successful motivation usually means providing a work climate that permits the employee to act in a manner that satisfies his own needs. Our knowledge of motivating is increasing daily, but there still remain many unknowns in this fascinating subject area. Agreement is usually voiced with the statement that every employee has a motivation response and this response can be fostered and utilized by managers creating opportunities, removing obstacles, providing guidance, and encouraging growth. The implementation or taking of actions, however, rests with the employee.

Figure 18 lists some basic concepts to remember in dealing with

---

1. People like to help others. Ask for their opinions.
2. People like to feel important and needed. Acknowledge their contribution and recognize their help occasionally in front of others.
3. People like to be encouraged. Help them see the successful accomplishment of their aims and ambitions.
4. People like good listeners. Let people talk about their accomplishments and disappointments. Give the other fellow a real hearing.
5. People like to be brought into the picture when talking about yourself. Give your conversation a "you" angle. "You will find this of special interest because. . . ."
6. People like a word of praise whenever merited.
7. People like a choice, if possible. Let a person decide for himself; help him reach conclusions, but do not make decisions for him.
8. People like to avoid embarrassment and being "boxed in a corner." Give a person an "out" and a chance to save face.
9. People like people who keep well groomed. Keep your body clean, clothes neat. This is a subtle way of saying to others, "I care about your opinion of me."
10. People like their image to be accepted. Strive to sense what this image is and let them know that you understand their picture of themselves.

FIG. 18.   In dealing with people, remember these concepts.

people. These concepts can be utilized in motivating employees, the application depending upon the particular circumstances in the individual case.

LEADERSHIP

Vital in supplying a motivating environment is leadership. People prefer to be with a successful leader. Being a part of victorious accomplishments, following a man who has demonstrated an ability to get things done, and having firsthand experience in observing successful management in action are in and of themselves highly motivating to an employee. Members of a group receive strong stimuli from effective leadership; and in turn, a strong leader acquires his position, in part, because of his ability to motivate members of his group.

What is leadership? It has been defined in a number of different ways;

but for our purposes here, we can consider that leadership implies a threefold meaning:

1. *Skill to direct—to show the way.* A leader possesses the ability to guide people—to point out the proper means for attainment. This leadership characteristic usually means that the leader is out in front leading, not in back pushing. While not directly applicable, the concept can be illustrated by considering a piece of ordinary wrapping twine. When the front end of the twine is directed and guided along desired paths, the rest of the piece of twine will follow. In contrast, when the twine is pushed, it follows no predetermined path and flounders in an aimless direction.

2. *Ability to win cooperation and loyalty.* A leader is able to get people to act jointly and to work toward a common goal. All efforts of the group are knit together and concentrated into one large force toward the attainment of the objective. This unity of operation is accomplished by strong and enthusiastic feelings, so that each member has a deep sense of obligation to the leader.

3. *Courage to carry on until the assigned task is accomplished.* A leader is dauntless and ever confident that the task to be done will be completely accomplished. He has implicit faith in the success of his actions and gives a feeling of confidence and positiveness to all associated with him.

People like to be led by a dynamic leader. They like to be led by a person who clearly envisages the goal, who knows how to achieve that goal, and who goes out after it. Once the decision is made as to what the goals are and what people must do to achieve them, leadership at all levels of the organization plays a dominant role in seeing that they are accomplished.

COMMUNICATION

High on the list of what to do to gain effective motivation is communication. Employees want to know what is going on and especially to be informed about achievements, problems, or changes that affect them. The normal tendency is to underrate the importance of communication. An aggressive and sincere communicative effort will do wonders toward achieving a cooperative, confident, and enthusiastic working force. An informed employee is usually a good employee. Employees like to be told firsthand about new policies and why they are being adopted, and they feel that they have a right to know about changes to be made in existing conditions.

Most difficulties of communication can be classified under the headings of either telling too little or assuming complete understanding of communication. Both of these habits tend to detract from our communication effectiveness. Managers should take the initiative and supply full information to employees. Dependence upon "word of mouth," or believing that "everybody knows that—it's common information," leads to incomplete and frequently incorrect information. The employee is eager to know any news in which he is involved. He wants to be informed, not coddled. Any information that will help him do a better job ranks high in his preference.

Tell an employee something you want him to understand, and the chances are 12 to 1 he will not fully understand you. Why is this? Because many believe that the act of writing or telling another certain information completely fulfills their job of communicating. However, to communicate effectively requires definite skills and knowledge. Included among these criteria are the following:

1. *Communication is two way.* One tells, informs, or requests; the other listens, asks, or interprets. Without listenership, the communication just does not exist. As Thoreau put it: "It takes two to speak the truth— one to speak, the other to hear it." Listening is an art and requires effort. For best results, involve the listener as soon as possible. Asking leading questions such as the following are effective: "How do you feel about . . . ?" "Well, what do you think—will it work?" "Now, what other information can I give you?"

2. *Think before you write or talk.* Some people are so intent on communicating that they start to write or talk before evaluating the situation and organizing their thoughts. As a result, they confuse the reader or listener. Before communicating, it is a good idea to decide: (1) Why do you want to say anything? (2) What do you want to say? (3) What is the objective in saying this? and (4) What do you know about the receiver or listener?

3. *Use effective words—focus words and mutually known words.* Focus words help to spot the key points in a communication. The listener or reader is assisted by phrases such as: "Our goal is to. . . ." or "To summarize, ..." These expressions aid in drawing inferences and value judgments. The use of mutually known words is essential. To describe the wage structure as "lucrative" reduces real communication if the receiver does not know the meaning of the word.

4. *Practice empathy.* Communication is assisted by the sender placing himself in the position of the receiver and judging the message from the receiver's point of view. This guide helps win acceptance by the receiver and emphasizes his interests, goals, and fears by giving the receiver what he wants to hear or read.

5. *Create a follow-up.* The recipient should be given the feeling that he can return with questions or ask clarification on any part he fails to understand. Offering assistance and closing with expressions such as: "Call me if any questions arise," or "Let's get together again next Monday noon and . . . ," are usually effective in this respect.

COMMUNICATION MEDIA

Normally, the formal lines of communication should be employed. These are the same connecting links as "lines of authority," discussed in Chapter 3. Organization shows relationships, and these relationships are

Medium	Features	Organizational Level for Which Effective
Conversation	Man-to-man, forthright personal relationship	All organizational levels
Letters	Excellent for statistical data and where permanent record is desired	Top managerial and supervisory levels
Pamphlets and booklets	Suitable for large volume of material	All organizational levels
House organs	Adequate coverage satisfactory for reminders and announcements	All organizational levels
Motion pictures, radio, and television	Dramatize presentation; helpful in training, relating company history, and special achievements	All organizational levels
Speeches	Impressive for special events and celebrations	Top managerial and supervisory levels

FIG. 19.   Media available for communication purposes.

made meaningful by exercise of both authority and communication. In fact, authority to put decisions into action necessitates communication. The traditional office grapevine is effective as a dispenser of information. It can never be completely eliminated, people and communication being what they are. The wise manager recognizes this and uses the grapevine as an auxiliary, but is exceedingly careful that accurate, complete, and timely messages are conveyed through the normal channels so that half-truths and incomplete information are not spread by the grapevine.

Many communication media are available. The selection depends chiefly upon the type of information and the type of employees to be reached. Figure 19 suggests the features and the organizational level for six selected media.

SUGGESTION SYSTEMS

A suggestion system is a means by which employees can submit their ideas to a manager and, if these ideas are adopted, receive an award, usually consisting of an amount of cash. Generally, the suggestions concern ways to save time, to reduce waste, to improve quality, or to simplify practices and procedures. A suggestion system can be a strong employee motivator because the employees are given the opportunity to say something, to feel that the company is "their company," to think of constructive ideas, and to contribute to the progress and betterment of the enterprise.

In addition, the economic gains can be quite large. Financial gains are made by the company as well as by the successful suggester. But these gains should not be stressed to the exclusion of the others mentioned. A suggestion system is far more than a mechanism for the buying of useful ideas.

Each and every suggestion should be answered promptly with reasons for decisions reached. Replies can be by individual letters or personal interviews; it is not a good practice to post lists on the bulletin board. Replies to turndowns, i.e., those suggestions receiving no award, must contain the reasons why such action is taken. This practice is recommended because it (1) lets the employee know that his suggestion was evaluated; (2) reveals whether the judging committee understood his idea; (3) helps him to become better informed, inasmuch as he is told why his idea was not worthy of an award; and (4) prompts him to continue to try and stimulates further thinking. The amount of the reward must be worthwhile and must offer some inducement to the employee. Many companies have found that $10 is a minimum figure to use and that maximum awards based on 10 percent of the savings for the first year are satisfactory.

Suggestion systems have a tendency to become dormant; for this reason, they must be continually promoted. Showmanship, publicity stunts, and promotions can be used to keep the program alive. Devices which have proved successful include the following: attractive suggestion forms; appealing and well-located suggestion boxes bearing the sign "Have you deposited your suggestion here today?"; attention-getting posters; reminders in payroll envelopes; and notices in company papers.

The suggester's identity is unknown to the investigator in some systems. This anonymity is obtained by means of a numbering and coupon arrangement on the suggestion form. The suggester retains a numbered coupon which corresponds to the number of the suggestion.

Under this arrangement, impartiality on the part of the investigators is promoted. In contrast, other systems require the suggester's signature, a practice which affords close contact with the suggester.

Suggestion stimulators can be directed to all employees in order to encourage their participation in the suggestion systems. Letters and announcements can be used; or more direct and definite means may be utilized, such as the manager asking: "What can you suggest to save time in the filing department?" Employees then start thinking of ways to improve that department. This practice appears to bring usable results, but it involves a serious disadvantage. It directs attention to fields foreign to the employee. A suggestion system is supposed to enable the employee to take advantage of the things he already knows but which have not as yet been used to full advantage. Directing his attention to new fields, therefore, might mean a loss of excellent ideas stemming from his intimate on-the-job knowledge.

MERIT RATING

Employees must be clear as to what is expected of them and how they are to be judged. This is a keystone of effective motivating. In addition, the typical employee wants the answer to the question: "How am I doing?" If highly successful, he would like to know it; if mediocre or even unsuccessful, he would like to know it, and why. Furthermore, it is motivating to him to know that his employer has an interest in him, is willing to give praise when deserved and to point out his shortcomings when existent, so that he can improve himself and satisfy his superior.

Merit rating, also commonly termed performance rating, should not be compared to the inspecting of a product on an assembly line. It is not an X ray of the employee. It is a two-way understanding between the employee and his supervisor involving the setting of objectives for the employee to develop himself and the means for achieving these objectives. Merit rating can be viewed as an inventory of the most valuable asset of the enterprise—its employees. Such efforts are essential to effective management; they constitute an important tool of managerial actuating and provide information helpful in many ways. Among the important uses of merit rating are:

1. To assist in developing the supervisor's critical evaluation of the employee's worth.
2. To provide a record of the progress of new employees or those in training.
3. To indicate areas where training is needed.

4. To let the employee know what management members think of his performance.

5. To uncover employees of unusual abilities along specific lines.

6. To guide personnel work in promoting, demoting, or transferring an employee.

7. To justify increases in wages within the established job range.

MERIT-RATING PLANS

Merit rating is accomplished by rating the employee on a number of predetermined factors. These factors are considered to be directly associated with, as well as indicative of, the employee's performance on the job. They should be carefully selected and include only those factors necessary to give adequate data. Usually, six to eight factors are sufficient, as the use of too many might lead to carelessness in rating, and too few might distort the ratings. Information which is available elsewhere, such as attendance, punctuality, and length-of-service data, should not be included in the merit-rating form. In each case, however, the factors selected are considered to be applicable to the employee, not to the job requirements.

There are four basic types of merit-rating plans: (1) employee comparison, (2) man-to-man basis, (3) check lists, and (4) charts. The first is an elementary form of ranking in which a comparison of the relative performance of employees is determined. Normally, the employees under a given supervisor or in one department are ranked, from the most satisfactory at the top of the list to the least satisfactory at the bottom of the list. The ranking can be by separate traits or on an overall basis.

In the man-to-man type, the employee is rated by comparing him to another employee believed to exemplify the highest rating of the particular factor being considered. Sometimes, a rating scale, established by the highest, middle, and lowest exemplary employees, respectively, is used. Thus, on the quality of dependability, for example, employee A is compared with each of the three employees included in the rating scale and is then given a rating it is believed he deserves. The man-to-man basis is not widely used in offices because it is rather complex and time-consuming. Difficulty is encountered in selecting the employees to use in the rating scale, and wide variations in the characteristics of those selected appear common.

Check lists consist of a series of statements or questions dealing with the employee's performance. Frequently, the statements have different values or weights which are unknown to the respondent. Questions which can be answered either "Yes" or "No," or by "It applies to this employee" or "It does not apply to this employee," are used. The following illustrates a portion of a check list:

Item	*Scale Value**
1. He works at a slow but steady pace...................	5
2. He is usually ahead of his work schedule...............	3
3. He gets along with fellow employees...................	8
4. He makes few mistakes in his work...................	10
5. He asks for considerable time off.....................	7
6. He usually thinks of the company first................	4

* Not included in form supplied to rater.

Charts are probably the most common type of merit rating used in an office. This is because they are easy to use, readily understood, and accepted by both the raters and the ratees. The chart type consists of a list of selected traits, each accompanied by a scale indicating different degrees of the trait. The rater indicates on each scale the extent to which the employee displays that respective trait in his work. For guidance to the rater, short descriptions for various degrees are usually provided. Figure 20 shows a performance-rating chart.

ADMINISTRATION OF MERIT RATING

Merit ratings are formally made about twice a year. The supervisor normally is charged with the responsibility of rating employees. Sometimes, assistance is given by his superior or by a member of the personnel department; and in some instances, several superiors who are in intimate contact with the employee rate him, in order that more than one judgment of his performance will be available. In most cases, the supervisor knows or should know most about the performance of the employee in his division or unit. Actually, no competent supervisor depends upon a rating form or waits for a given time of the year to appraise his employee. It is a continuous job. Formal and periodic merit rating helps codify results and insures that some orderly appraisal is taking place.

An interview between the employee and the management representative affords an opportunity for a forthright discussion on the employee's performance. Each factor of the merit rating can be discussed in a constructive and factual manner. Recognition of the employee as an individual can be increased and employee good will be enhanced. The interview can be highly objective, because preplanning and concentration upon specific topics are feasible.

Employee self-appraisal is another helpful technique. When office

BLUE CROSS - BLUE SHIELD PLANS
CHICAGO

PERFORMANCE RATING

NAME:_____   DATE of RATING:_____

DEPARTMENT:_____   JOB CLASSIFICATION:_____

JOB KNOWLEDGE	How Well Does This Employee Understand The Requirements Of Job To Which Assigned:					
	Thoroughly understands all aspects of job.	More than adequate knowledge of job.	Has sufficient knowledge to do job.	Insufficient knowledge of some phases.	Continually needs instruction.	
QUALITY OF WORK	How Accurate, Neat And Complete Is The Work:					
	Consistently neat, accurate and thorough.	Careful worker seldom needs correction.	Work is acceptable.	Occasionally Careless —needs checking.	Inaccurate and careless.	
CO-OPERATION	Does This Employee Work Harmoniously And Effectively With Co-Workers And Supervision:					
	Exceptionally willing and successful as a team worker.	Usually tactful and offers to assist others.	Gets along well enough, no problem.	Cooperation must be solicited, seldom volunteers.	Tends to be a troublemaker.	
RESPONSIBILITY	How Does This Employee Accept All The Responsibilities Of The Job:					
	Accepts all responsibilities fully and meets Emergencies.	Conscientiously tries to fulfill job responsibilities.	Accepts but does not seek responsibility.	Does some assigned tasks reluctantly.	Indifferent—avoids responsibilities.	
INITIATIVE	How Well Does This Employee Begin An Assignment Without Direction And Recognize The Best Way Of Doing It:					
	Self starter: makes practical suggestions.	Proceeds on assigned work voluntarily and readily accepts suggestions.	Does regular work without prompting.	Relies on others: needs help getting started.	Must usually be told exactly what to do.	
QUANTITY OF WORK	How Much Satisfactory Work Is Consistently Turned Out By This Employee:					
	Maintains unusually high out-put.	Usually does more than expected.	Does sufficient amount of work.	Inclined to be slow.	Inadequate turn-out of work.	
DEPENDABILITY	How Faithful Is This Employee In Reporting To Work And Staying On The Job:					
	Places company interests ahead of personal conveniences.	Punctual and does not waste company time.	Generally on the job as needed.	Some abuses — occasionally needs to be admonished.	Chronic abuses of working schedules.	

COMMENTS:_____

_____

_____

Rated By:_____   Discussed With Employee: By___._____

Is any action being taken to help this employee improve his performance? ☐ No ☐ Yes—Specify_____

_____

_____   Dept. Manager_____

RB—9-7-59   (See Reverse Side For Instructions in Rating)

Courtesy: Blue Cross–Blue Shield Plans, Chicago

FIG. 20. An effective performance-rating chart.

employees are fully informed in advance of the purpose, operation, and application of merit rating, they make remarkably accurate self-appraisals. There is some tendency, however, for the better employees to underrate themselves, and the problem employees may overrate themselves. Employee self-appraisal helps to give the *how* and *why* of merit rating to the employee. He knows what is expected of him and uncovers areas in which improvements can be made. Self-analysis encourages self-development. Self-appraisals can be recorded on special forms provided for this purpose. They supplement the regular ratings determined by management-designated raters.

Since judgment and subjective factors are important in merit rating, it is advisable to supply a training program for raters in order to help secure intelligent and well-considered ratings. Training helps to implement the plan properly and constructively. The rater must understand the purpose of the form and what method to follow. Competent rating work is a key area of satisfactory merit rating. Also, it is important to provide retraining periodically, so that new developments in employee-rating work and future plans can be brought to the attention of the raters. A retraining program also aids in reviewing the principles of good rating with each rater before each rating period.

Review by a management panel is highly successful in many companies. Funneling all ratings within an enterprise through one body makes for better control and greater uniformity of ratings. Employees who are qualified for promotions, transfers, training, and salary increases are readily identified. Likewise, those requiring remedial action are identified, and proper measures can be taken.

In administering merit rating the following considerations warrant attention:

1. Top management backing for merit rating is essential to its success.

2. Merit rating should serve primarily to motivate employees, to inventory personnel, and to improve the working force.

3. The rating form should include only those traits that cannot be measured objectively by standard personnel records.

4. Only those traits of greatest importance to an employee's progress should be utilized; usually, eight to ten traits are adequate.

5. To expedite comparisons and the rating work, rate all employees on one trait, then all on the second trait, and so forth.

6. Normally, and in keeping with statistical probability, of the ratings for many on a single trait, a few will be low, a few will be high, and the greatest number, perhaps 60 percent, will be average.

7. Each trait should be a single one, not compound; should be defined

objectively, not subjectively; and should be in terms of work performed on the job.

8. Ratings should be based on observations of definite and concrete actions.

9. Ratings of an employee should be discussed with him in private by the rater.

10. Periodic training and retraining of raters are essential for success of a merit-rating program.

PROMOTIONS, ABSENTEEISM, AND TARDINESS

Promotions are motivating in that they afford satisfaction to the average individual in his desire to develop, to advance, and to improve his status. Most companies have the policy of promoting from among their present employees whenever possible. This requires keeping a sharp eye open for the discovery of promotable personnel—those people who demonstrate a desire to advance by qualifying for a better and more responsible job. Qute a few managers, however, feel that some of the vacancies for better jobs should be filled by candidates from outside the enterprise. By this means, it is contended, new ideas, new attitudes, and different methods of operation are brought in which tend to foster an active, healthy condition.

The initiative for promotion work belongs with the manager. Without prodding, the manger should see that worthy people are promoted. The knowledge of whom to advance is gained through records covering each employee's merit, competence, and length of service. Actually, promotion implies two-way action. It calls for action by the managers—to open up avenues along which employees can advance; and it calls for action by employees—to qualify themselves for advancement.

The failure of an employee to report on the job when scheduled to work is one of the difficult personnel problems with which the average office manager must cope. Absenteeism disrupts the smooth flow of work; either the work stops completely, or extra work is forced upon another employee. There is no single cure for absenteeism. It is an individual problem and the correction must suit the particular case. Records revealing who is absent, how long, how often, and why give information on where to concentrate corrective efforts.

Among the various motivating means used to reduce absenteeism are pointing out to employees the importance of being on the job, talking with each absentee upon return and thoroughly discussing the cause and explanation offered, checking to see if the right person is on the right job, maintaining a continued health program, allowing a definite number of days off per year, requiring absentees to make up time, and showing some outward thanks and appreciation to those employees who are always on the job.

Bad timekeeping on the part of employees indicates a disrespect for others and a lack of dependability. Tardiness is contagious. When one or two continue to come into the office late, the idea gets in the minds of other employees that such behavior has managerial approval. Being early is as much a habit as being late. The hour at which work starts has little influence on the problem. The tendency to procrastinate must be corrected and the importance of keeping time obligations stressed.

An effective motivating means consists of creating a strong employee interest in promptness. Supervisors should set good examples and always be on time themselves. They should also keep reminding the employees about the importance of being on time. In many instances, the employee simply fails to allow himself sufficient time to get ready for work. Dependence upon hairline transportation connections and failure to allow extra time for travel under bad weather conditions are common causes. The means of correction here are self-evident.

In many offices, a tardy employee is required to report first to the office manager or to the timekeeper, where an explanation is given verbally for the tardiness and a form filled out indicating the reason why. The idea of going through a "lot of red tape" helps discourage tardiness. The imposition of a penalty, such as making up time lost or doing the least desirable work, proves effective. However, before using such a plan, it should meet the approval of the employees, who should agree to "go along with it." One company uses a unique plan which brings surprisingly good results. An employee's name is selected at random from the payroll list; and promptly at starting time, the employee is called on the telephone. If he answers, indicating presence and promptness on the job, he receives a reward of $20.

EMPLOYEE ECONOMIC SECURITY

Various arrangements are now available to help provide a measure of economic security to employees. These arrangements have a motivating influence and are beneficial in that they assist in supplying economic aid in case of sickness or old age. Also, at the time of death some help is given dependents of the deceased employee. These economic security measures have been brought about through the efforts of companies and employees and the influence of state and federal laws, among which are unemployment insurance regulations, workmen's compensation laws, and social security regulations. The form, purpose, and content of these various plans vary considerably and require special study for complete understanding.

The discussion here will be confined to three arrangements, including:

1. *Hospitalization plans.* These plans are a form of insurance which pays a portion of hospital expenses resulting from all nonoccupational illnesses or accidents suffered by the employee. Premiums are usually paid by the employee, although in some instances the company contributes toward the plan. Under a typical plan, costs might be $10 per month for an unmarried employee for semiprivate accommodations. The amount of cost varies with such factors as the number of employees in the plan, their sex and age, and the benefits provided.

2. *Pension plans.* These provide regular payments to an employee retired from service. The great majority of large enterprises now have such plans. They make it possible not only to give needed relief and to grant rewards for long service but also to retire older employees, thus permitting the employment of younger persons as replacements. This helps keep the work force alive and vibrant, and the existence of a retirement pension plan makes for high morale and attracts better employees.

The cost of a pension plan can be paid by either the company or the employees, or both. The amount of retirement pay generally provided is about 50 percent of the average rate for the five-year period preceding retirement. The trend is toward a reduction in the waiting period for eligibility and the elimination of high age requirements of participants for pensions. Programs under which the employee contributes are also becoming more common. The plan should be based on a sound actuarial basis. It is usually advisable to employ the services of specialists in this field.

3. *Group insurance plans.* Protection for individual employees as members of a group is provided by group insurance plans. Usually, employees are eligible only after a stipulated period of service and in an amount relative to their earnings. The company or the employees may pay the full cost of the plan, or the cost may be assumed jointly. Employees are usually able to secure protection at a cost below that of individually purchased insurance of the same protection. The exact nature of the policy varies with different plans; the basis of all is straight life insurance coverage, but this frequently is supplemented with other benefits.

EMPLOYEES' RECREATIONAL ACTIVITIES

Recreational activities have motivating influence, but they also help provide a balance between work and play. A well-rounded program of recreational activities is an important part of personnel activities because it improves employer-employee relations, increases efficiency, and makes for healthy, satisfied employees. Such activities may include the following: archery, baseball, softball, basketball, tennis, horseback riding, golf, bowling, horseshoe pitching, swimming, hiking, band, glee club, photography club, and amateur shows.

The participation of management members in recreational activities should consist of a readiness to furnish advice, to offer suggestions, and to lend assistance *upon request*. Managers should not attempt to force inclusion of certain activities or to run the program. Any semblance of paternalism should be avoided.

In guiding the development of the program, the following approach is usually helpful:

1. Measure the adequacy of the activity to find out the total number of employees who can participate.

2. Examine each existing activity to see if it is attracting a capacity number of employees.

3. Investigate public and private recreational facilities to determine how and when they can be used.

4. Find out what is included in programs of other companies.

5. Publicize the existence of the activities so that all employees who can and want to participate may do so.

SUGGESTIONS FOR EFFECTIVE MOTIVATING

Certain general guides which, in many offices, have proved successful in motivating employees will now be given. To some extent, these are a review of what has already been stated; but in the following form, they can prove helpful and convenient.

1. *Believe in yourself and in other people.* Effective motivating starts with a genuine belief both in yourself as a management member and in the people under your direction. A manager must sincerely believe that he can motivate and must want to motivate his employees. Belief in employees means thinking and promoting the idea that they can plan

better, exercise authority better, and do their work better, and giving them the opportunity to do so.

2. *Set a good example.* The management member should demonstrate by his actions the kind of effort he would like his employees to exert. Performance on the part of the leader, his attitude, and his work habits tend to set a pattern which employees copy. Important in this consideration is to keep busy—everyone, including the supervisor, should have enough meaningful work to do. Failure to provide ample work results sooner or later in employee dissatisfaction and a lack of justification for the money spent in their employment.

3. *Place employees in proper jobs.* Employees normally will give their best efforts in work they like and feel competent to perform. They need to have assignments they are capable of performing. Finding the field of endeavor best suited for each individual employee's capacity and interest, as well as following up to insure that each member is on the best job for which he is currently adapted, will assist in stimulating the employee's best efforts.

4. *Stress participation.* Rare indeed is the person motivated to unusual achievement without some participation in the planning, discussion, and decision making of the activity in which he is going to take a part. Actually, this is a basis for practicing delegation of authority.[1] An employee wants to say something about conditions that affect him. Employees want to be asked their opinions about factors involving their work. They appreciate an audience. By such means, the employee gains the feeling that his employer has an interest in, and cares about, those working for him. Likewise, the desire "to get ahead"—to advance, to win status and prestige—tends to be satisfied when participation is stressed. In some companies, weekly meetings among members of a department are held in order to bring the employees into the task of operating the department by seeking their counsel.

5. *Keep employees informed.* It is a natural human tendency to want to know what is going on, why this or that operation is important, and what changes are being considered—in short, to be kept informed. This adds to an employee's sense of belonging and of being an integral part of the organizational structure. Employees want to feel they are valued members of the team. Communicating effectively with people is essential in motivating them.

6. *Give adequate incentive and reward.* This can and does take many different forms including the amount of wages, the granting of special privileges, the conferring of titles, and the instilling of competition

---

[1] See Chapter 3.

between departments or among employees. To illustrate, the amount of compensation, as well as a proper differential between jobs, is important. Employees want comparable pay for comparable jobs, and salaries that are "in line" with those of other enterprises in the area. They may be less interested in the amount of their own pay than in the relationship of their pay to that of other employees. Individual recognition, awarding of honors, and seniority can be cited as common means of granting special privileges, but these rewards are conferred within the limits of well-publicized policies. Employees can be greatly motivated when the reward offered has significant value to them.

7. *Recognize achievements of employees.* Most employees want to feel useful; they want their efforts to be appreciated. In short, they want recognition. Credit where credit is due and a sincere expression of satisfaction from the employer for a job well done are effective motivating means. The practice of holding periodic talks in private with each employee is also highly recommended. In this way, the employee is individualized, he is afforded recognition, he can voice his feelings about aspects of his job, and a better employer-employee understanding can be established.

8. *Develop group spirit.* Motivation is assisted by making employees feel they are a part of the group and are needed on the team. In this respect, various employee recreational activities can be used to good advantage. The group spirit among an interested and participating number of employees is also fostered by giving them certain facts and an objective, then letting them, as a team, come up with a recommended course of action. In one company, the employees are given a profit and loss statement based on the work they performed and are requested to tie this in with the major objectives of the company.

9. *Give information about the job itself.* To be motivated effectively, each employee must believe his work is wholesome and important. The relationship of his assignment to the entire office and to the aims of the company should be clearly brought out. It is helpful to point out why the particular equipment and machines are supplied so that an attitude of pride in performing work well and in being a part of the enterprise is developed.

10. *Provide an opportunity for job security.* Almost every employee is concerned about having steady work—not being laid off or losing his job. Security is the main reason for demanding restrictions on the type of work that an employee can perform. Also, adequate financial support for old age or to take care of illness or accidents is an important security want of the employee. Providing this wanted security can have a stimulating effect upon the employee. However, it is necessary to keep him aware

of it and to point out that work accomplishments effectively attained are the best means of achieving and maintaining job security.

11. *Employ fear judiciously.* Fear is a negative force; but when properly used, it can serve as a very strong motivator. The apprehension of not wanting certain happenings to take place can cause a person to exert unusually strong efforts in the direction away from the unwanted event.

12. *Exercise strong leadership.* All normal persons are motivated by competent leaders. The typical employee wants a leader who knows what he is doing, can speak authoritatively, never makes promises he cannot keep, builds confidence, and takes prompt disciplinary action whenever necessary.

RESEARCH IN ACTUATING OFFICE EMPLOYEES

Why is the successful actuating of office employees one of the most helpful of all managerial skills? The answer, in part, is because typically the office employee calls upon only a fraction of his full potentiality in performing his job. Managers commonly do not tap the ultimate of what an employee is capable of doing. The main reason is because available motivating tools and their application are inadequate. Much more needs to be known about motivating and how to apply it.

It is hoped that research will supply the answer. Research is a lucrative source of new techniques, new methods, and new information. It seeks to appraise by objective means. It strives to answer such questions as "How well is the job now being done?" "Can it be improved?" and "What will create more interest in performing their work?"

Good research starts with basic factual knowledge about each employee. Included are records of what motivating techniques were used and the results obtained from each. Evaluation of results in order to codify relationships between application and accomplishments is essential. In addition, adequate and complete personnel records are necessary. Success in providing such records depends chiefly upon the content and number of records used, the accuracy of the recorded data, and the analysis and interpretation given them. Available standardized personnel forms will be found helpful, but these should be reviewed in terms of what is essential for the particular program. Among the more common records are: personnel history of the employee; employee's application form; physical examination findings; results of selection tests; identification record; data on training; merit ratings; seniority ratings; safety record; first-aid record; record of attendance, warnings, and demerits; salary and earnings; and termination.

In addition, a personnel record folder on each employee is very helpful. This folder consists of a collection of all personnel records pertaining to the employee; it gives the complete story on that employee and makes this information available for instant reference. Normally, it contains the records listed above; but in some cases, either more or less records may be retained.

CHAPTER SIX

OFFICE SALARY

ADMINISTRATION

*That man is truly free who desires what he is able
to perform, and does what he desires.*
—Rousseau

Compensation is motivating to an employee. Man does not work for money alone but for what he can do with the money he receives. Fundamental are his needs for food, clothing, and shelter and the challenge to satisfy these needs is motivating; but after providing adequately for them, man seeks to fulfill other wants and takes on tasks and seeks compensation sufficient to satisfy these other wants. Hence, the monetary reward for performing work is a fundamental consideration in actuating and helps get work accomplished that otherwise might not be accomplished.

ADMINISTRATION OF COMPENSATION

There are a myriad of influences affecting office salary administration. At any given time some factors are tending to push salaries up while others are having the directly opposite effect. And these respective forces are of varying degrees. The subject of compensating can become quite complicated. To simplify our discussion, we will identify three considerations which are normally of major significance in the office area. These include (1) salary surveys, (2) salary differentials, and (3) salary patterns.

Salary surveys are conducted to find out what enterprises are paying so that you can keep your salaries competitive and in line. Great care must be taken to make certain that valid comparisons are being made. As pointed out previously, one of the greatest sources of error involves identical job titles, with wide differences in job content. Likewise, what is actually being produced may differ. For example, in company "A" an accounting machine operator may be paid $95 a week and perform 20 transactions an hour whereas in company "B" an accounting machine operator is paid $95 a week and performs 16 transactions an hour. Is a comparison between the two $95-a-week salaries truly meaningful? Salary surveys are helpful but not conclusive. Frequently they are performed by a trade association, a professional society, an organization of manufacturers, or similar enterprises. Each participating company receives a copy of the results, which are coded to mask the sources.

Salary differentials exist and are justifiable because job requirements differ. Work that requires higher knowledge and skill normally commands a higher salary than work requiring lower knowledge and skill. That salary differentials should exist is generally accepted; the real question is, "What differential is fair and just?" In addition, wage differentials exist between different geographical areas. Office salaries in San Francisco, for example, are higher than those in Memphis. Furthermore, office salaries for the same type of office work can vary within San Francisco. A typist for an import-export firm may receive less salary than a typist in a San Francisco bank.

Salary patterns tend to be formulated by the leading enterprise or enterprises in an area and in many instances these patterns are adopted by other enterprises in the area. This follow-the-leader practice can be extremely rigid or somewhat flexible, in which case the leader enterprise can have an influence, but its policies and practices may not be adopted in totality. Leader or pilot enterprises, however, usually in some degree affect salary administration actions and constitute an influence with which to reckon.

Job evaluation, or some adaptation of it, is used by most office managers to keep office salaries paid in line with what others are paying for similar work, to provide proper wage differentials, and to be competitive salarywise. In addition to job evaluation, the core of most office salary administration programs includes consideration of how well the incumbent is doing the particular job, regard for the amount paid for "fringe benefits," and recognition of certain social and economic influences. Each of these will be discussed. We will start with job evaluation.

JOB EVALUATION

The concept of the job and its relative worth are considered in job evaluating, which can be formally defined as follows: *Job evaluation is the determination of the relative value of each individual job in an enterprise and is arrived at by means of a systematic procedure using jobs or selected job factors for comparison or measurement.* There are four main methods of carrying out job evaluation work, including (1) ranking, (2) classification, (3) factor comparison, and (4) point.

1. *Ranking Method.* The jobs within an enterprise can be arranged according to their relative difficulty. A ranking of the jobs is thus obtained; and in this manner, the relative importance of each one is established. The job at the top of the list has the highest value, and the job at the bottom of the list has the lowest value. The usual procedure is (1) to rank the jobs in an individual department and (2) to combine all departmental rankings into one composite ranking.

Figure 21 illustrates the results which might be obtained from this

ARRAY OF JOBS ACCORDING TO RANKING METHOD

Rank No.	Name of Job	Earnings per Week*
1	Accounting clerk I	$120
2	Purchasing clerk	116
3	Traffic clerk I	112
4	Cashier	108
5	Accounting clerk II	104
6	Traffic clerk II	100
7	Cost clerk	96
8	Tabulating-machine operator	92
9	General bookkeeper	88
10	Correspondent	84
11	Stenographer	80
12	Switchboard operator	76
13	Typist I	72
14	File clerk	68
15	Typist II	64
16	Office boy	60

* In uniform variation from top to bottom.

FIG. 21.

method. For example, the job of "accounting clerk I" was considered of greater value than the job of "purchasing clerk," while the job of "office boy" was ranked lowest in the office. If the weekly salary of the top job is set at $120 and that of the lowest job at $60, then the rank order of the intermediate jobs, assuming a straight-line or uniform variation, is shown in the last column in the illustration.

2. *Classification Method.* Under this method, a predetermined number of job classes or groups are established, and the jobs are assigned to

these classifications. For example, the job classes, from highest to lowest, might include:

Class A. Executive
  Office manager
  Office departmental supervisor
Class B. Skilled
  Purchasing clerk
  Traffic clerk
  Cashier
Class C. Limited skilled
  Tabulating-machine operator
  Stenographer
  Switchboard operator
Class D. Unskilled
  File clerk
  Office boy

In this method, the jobs within each grade frequently must be graded further to show more adequately the existing relationships. To do this, the ranking method, previously described, can be employed.

3. *Factor Comparison Method.* Jobs can also be evaluated according to predetermined factors which have been established as a measure of ranking. Customarily, a key-job comparison scale is established and used for this purpose. Job factors are listed across the top and the dollars per week or salary-rating schedule in the left column. The scale provides the means for applying *salary rates* to job relatives as needed.

Assume four job factors: education, experience, responsibility, and working conditions. On each of these factors, each key job is ranked. Generally, eight to ten jobs are considered key jobs, selected on the basis of the jobs requiring widely different amounts of the job factors being utilized. To illustrate, for the "accounting clerk I" job, the rating values given for each of the job factors might be:

Education.....................................$ 36.00
Experience.................................... 28.00
Responsibility................................ 44.00
Working conditions........................... 12.00
  Total.....................................$120.00

In other words, from the key-job comparison scale, it is possible to determine what portion of the present salary of a job is being paid for each factor.

This scale is the measuring device for evaluating all other jobs in the company. Other jobs are fitted into this scale, with the key-job evaluations being used as guides. To illustrate, consider the job of "tabulating-

4. Responsibility for Loss

Level	LEVEL DEFINITION	Points
A	Nature of work involves negligible opportunity for loss. Normal or reasonable care required and all work is verified or proved by repeating entire operation.	3
B	Nature of work is such that more than normal or reasonable care is required to prevent loss. However, work is checked by proving against totals or some standard rather than by repetition of operation.	15
C	Nature of work involves moderate but constant opportunity for error, limited only by daily or subsequent spot check or examination. Great care should be exercised to prevent loss. Potential serious loss from errors in transcription or computation.	27
D	Good judgment must be exercised regularly to prevent loss. Work is of such nature that complete and correct performance is hard to control, reliance being placed on the individual. Work subject to general supervision and occasional review.	38
E	Work of such a nature that commitments are made which may involve the entire bank. Work is frequently released without any check being made or is checked only by individual doing the work. A high degree of financial responsibility is involved.	50

Courtesy: J. D. Moore Organization, Park Ridge, Ill.

FIG. 22.   Illustrating the different levels of "responsibility for loss" and the number of points assigned to each level.

machine operator." The evaluator would first read the job analysis sheet for this job. Then, concentrating his attention on the factor of education, he judges where under the education column the job of tabulating-machine operator seems to fit. He might decide that this job requires a little more education than a certain key job but less than another key job. Hence, he would evaluate "tabulating-machine operator" between the two considered key jobs. In similar manner, the job is evaluated according to the other job factors, and the other jobs in the company are evaluated in a similar manner.

4. *Point Method.* In this method, job factors are selected, and each is assigned a maximum number of points or credits. The selection of job factors is qualified by the following: that each job factor (1) exists in all the jobs to be evaluated, (2) varies in amount in the different jobs to be evaluated, and (3) is mutually exclusive of other job factors. The maximum point value assigned to each factor is determined by its relative importance. This is governed primarily by the judgment and experience of the analyst. Normally, from eight to fourteen factors are used. Those most common include skill, experience, education, responsibilities, working conditions, effort, and supervisory requirements.

Each selected job factor is defined in clear and simple language. The degree or intensity of each selected factor is broken down, and points are assigned for each level of the factor. Figure 22 shows these data for the factor "responsibility for loss," which has been given five levels, *A* through *E*, ranging in value from a low of 3 to a maximum of 50 points. Figure 23 illustrates 11 job factors selected for use in the evaluation of clerical and supervisory jobs. In this case, the data showing the level and the points of rating, along with pertinent comments for the job of "junior accountant," are indicated for each factor. Note that under factor No. 4, "responsibility for loss," the rating level of *B* is valued at 15 points, which was arrived at by referring to the guide shown by Figure 22.

PRICING THE JOB

The ultimate aim of job evaluation is to determine the job price or rate of pay. Jobs of high evaluation should command high rates of pay; in general, the higher the evaluation, the higher the pay. The immediate problem is to determine what the rate of pay should be when the evaluation is a known amount. The job prices to be established must be consistent (1) externally (rates within the enterprise are in line with the rates paid outside the enterprise) and (2) internally (rates within the enterprise are directly associated within the evaluations).

External consistency is accomplished by securing the current wage rates in the area from salary surveys conducted by enterprises specializing in this type of work or from local governmental offices. Sometimes, to supplement available information, a thorough salary survey must be made. It is also well to remember that accurate job descriptions and productivity data add greatly to the usefulness of salary survey results.

Internal consistency is determined by comparing the job evaluations

CODE .... SALARY GRADE .... VI ....

JOB TITLE .... JUNIOR ACCOUNTANT ....

CLERICAL AND SUPERVISORY EVALUATION

	NO.	FACTOR	RATING LEVEL	RATING PTS.	JOB REQUIREMENT
SKILL	1	Essential Knowledge	D	84	Requires a knowledge of advanced accounting methods and procedures and a working knowledge of company financial policies.
	2	Experience and Training	G	73	Normally requires 3 to 5 years' training and experience, including 2 years' accounting training plus 3 years' company experience as an Accounting Clerk.
	3	Analytical Requirements	C	27	Requires analysis of figures and data which vary in content but follow general patterns of application
RESPONSIBILITY	4	Responsibility For Loss	B	15	Requires more than normal care to prevent loss due to miscalculations. However, work is usually checked against totals.
	5	Confidential Information	B	6	Involves preparation and use of limited confidential matters in the Accounting Department.
	6	Contacts Public and Internal	B	28	Involves routine contacts with persons where detailed subject matter must be presented satisfactorily.
	7	Individual Initiative	B	12	Involves initiative in planning details of own work.
EFFORT	8	Mental Effort	C	15	Requires moderate mental effort to solve problems of accounting.
	9	Physical Effort	A	6	Involves light physical effort with intermittent standing and sitting at comfortable intervals.
	10	Work Conditions	A	0	Working conditions are excellent.
	11	Supervisory Requirements	FX	18	Involves immediate leadership over Accounting Clerks and Typists.
		TOTAL POINTS		284	

Courtesy: J. D. Moore Organization, Park Ridge, Ill.

FIG. 23. Job factors, ratings, and comments for the job of "junior accountant."

with the rates paid. In some cases, this can be done by a simple comparison of columnar data. Very often, however, a graphic representation helps to visualize this comparison, especially when the point system of evaluation has been used. Commonly employed is a chart or scatter diagram in which existent wage rates are plotted on the vertical

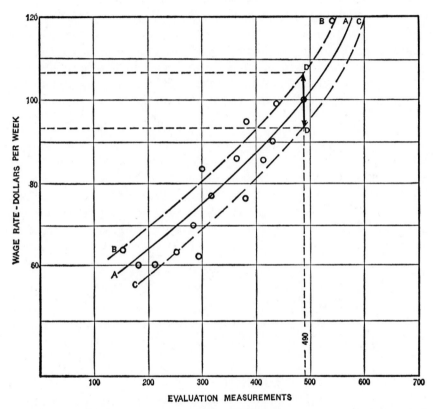

FIG. 24. Scatter diagram showing relationship between wage rates and evaluation measurements.

axis and evaluations on the horizontal axis. A curve showing consistent relationships between rates and evaluations can then be drawn on the chart. The deviations of actual rates from this curve can readily be spotted, and jobs overpaid or underpaid with respect to their evaluation can be quickly observed.

Figure 24 is a scatter diagram showing the relationship between wage rates and evaluations. The plotted points are indicated by the small circles. Curve *AA* has been drawn in and represents what is considered to be a consistent relationship between rates and evaluations. Curves *BB* and *CC* have been drawn in for reasons discussed in the paragraphs that follow.

JOB PRICE RANGE

From a practical viewpoint, the office manager is interested in more than a job price for each job. What he really wants is (1) *a price range for each job,* not a single price for each job; and (2) *a price range to cover a group of jobs,* not just one job. A price range provides flexibility and makes for a better salary plan. Furthermore, when a group of jobs are within one price range, the entire task of wage determination is simplified.

Referring again to Figure 24, a wage range has been indicated by the two curves *BB* and *CC* drawn on the chart.[1] The job of "traffic clerk II," for example, evaluated at 490 points, has a range from $93 to $107 per week, indicated by ordinate *DD* on the chart.

To provide a group of jobs within one price range, it is customary to group jobs into classes so that all jobs in the same class have the same price range. In other words, jobs of the same worth are put into the same class. The number of job classes depends primarily upon the total number of jobs, and the spread between the highest and the lowest job. Usually, a total of six to ten job classes is sufficient in most offices.

As already discussed, the classification method of job evaluation automatically puts the jobs into various classes. On the other hand, when any of the other methods of job evaluation are used, the alignment of jobs is arbitrarily divided into different numbers and levels or classes.

ADVANTAGES OF JOB EVALUATION

A solid foundation for an office salary administration is supplied by job evaluation because it (1) shows the relative value of office jobs within a company, (2) assists in the evaluating of new office jobs, (3) helps obtain a satisfactory wage level for all office jobs within the company, (4) helps to eliminate salary inequalities by putting office jobs having similar requirements in the same salary range, and (5) affords factual data for the settling of salary disputes. It is imperative, however, that the work of determining job content, grades, and price ranges be kept up to date by

---

[1] Frequently, a constant percentage change from the center line is used to establish the outside range lines. For example, for $50 median, the range is $45–$55; for $90 median, the range is $81–$99.

regular, periodic checkups. The content of many jobs changes in the normal course of events; and this, in turn, frequently changes the relative values of the jobs. Likewise, changes in the general wage levels appear to be the usual rather than the exceptional happenings.

HOW WELL THE INCUMBENT IS DOING HIS JOB

Up to this point we have confined our discussion to what the job is worth. Let us now consider an equally important concept in office salary administration, namely, how well the incumbent is doing his job. For this purpose, merit rating, discussed in the previous chapter, is commonly used. In some programs, merit rating tempered with seniority is followed. The justification for this approach is that the employee who has been on the job for a long period tends to perform the work better or at least knows more about how it should be performed. This viewpoint, however, is open to question, but in offices where it is followed, it is usually popular and brings quite satisfactory results.

Bonus arrangements are employed by some companies to demonstrate approval of satisfactory office work accomplishments. Usually the payments of bonuses commemorate special occasions, such as Christmas, a birthday, or an employment anniversary. These payments commonly amount to sizable sums—perhaps an extra month's pay or, in some cases, as much as 20 percent of a year's salary. They are given to share the results of profitable operations, to recognize outstanding service, to continue a traditional custom, or to improve employee morale.

Financial incentive plans are another means of recognizing how well the incumbent is doing. These plans provide for total compensation based to some extent on the amount of work accomplished instead of strictly on the basis of time spent at work. Generally speaking, financial incentive plans are not common in offices, but their use is growing. The more common incentive office work includes transcribing, card punching, order processing, and billing.

FUNDAMENTALS OF OFFICE INCENTIVE PLANS

There are two fundamental concepts in practically all office incentive plans: (1) a base or standard amount of work output and (2) the amount of wage payment which will be given for production below standard, at standard, or above standard. The first concept, the base amount of work output, can be determined by past performance records, by time studies, or by guess. Customarily, this standard amount of work is expressed as

100 percent. The amount of work which is established as standard is extremely important, for it is commonly, but not always, the point at which the incentive pay begins. The second concept, or pattern of the amount of wage payment, varies with the incentive plan. Some plans guarantee base rates up to standard; others do not. Some divide the excess above standard equally between employee and employer, while others share the overflow according to various percentages.

The same general type of plan can be used for a group as for a single employee. The group can be used when the nature of the work is such that its segregation among individual employees is very difficult or costly. The group incentive pay is figured first, than divided among the members according to either the individual base wage rates, the number of hours worked by each member, the individual gross base pay, or on some other agreed basis.

Incentive wage plans should be tailor-made to suit the particular office and to achieve the particular objectives desired from the plan. The following guides are helpful:

1. Incentive plans should have the backing of the top managers.

2. The best incentive plan is usually the simple plan. It should be thoroughly understood by all concerned.

3. There should be a close relationship between reward (incentive pay) and results (contribution).

4. An incentive based on the individual employee is generally better than one based on a group.

5. The work output should increase as well as the amount of salaries.

6. The base or standard production amounts should be carefully determined—preferably by measured time studies.

7. The number of temporary standards should be held to a minimum. When standards are temporary, this fact should be known to all concerned.

8. The incentive wage should be neither guaranteed nor limited. In most instances, the base wage should be guaranteed.

9. The standards should be reviewed for possible revision whenever any change is made in the material, machine, or method used.

10. If indirect production employees, such as messenger boys, receptionists, and telephone operators, are included in the plan, they should be affiliated on some measurable basis, such as the maintenance of an acceptable ratio between the total indirect man-hours to the total direct man-hours, or the total indirect man-hours to total work output. This tends to keep the indirect man-hours under control.

FRINGE BENEFITS

Another major area of modern office salary administration is fringe benefits. These include (1) legally required benefits—social security, unemployment, workmen's compensation requirements, (2) pay *away* from the job—paid leaves, vacations, and holidays, (3) pay *on* the job for time off—employee meetings, overtime pay, and shift premium pay, and (4) special benefits—service awards, meal allowances, relocation expenses, and tuition aid. Various estimates point to an average of about 28 percent of total base payroll costs constituting expense for fringe benefits. The trend in the amount of fringe benefits has been steadily upward during the last decade. Wage experts predict fringe benefits will represent 40 percent of payroll costs by 1980.

Many office employees give considerable weight to the fringe benefits included in a job. The dollar "take home" pay is adjusted in view of the fringe benefits received; and it is common to find an office employee preferring to work for a particular concern where the dollar salaries are average or even low, but the numerous fringe benefits provided make for an attractive total remuneration.

A big need in the fringe benefits area is for employers to explain and publicize their benefit programs. Too frequently complicated mathematical formulas and legal phraseology are communicated in response to simple employee questions. As a rule, employees want simple answers, not problems. They want to know their benefit position. What is available to an employee and his dependents if and when an emergency arises is what he wants to know. The wise office manager tells him in language that he can understand.

SOCIAL AND ECONOMIC INFLUENCES

Last of the major areas of office salary administration discussed here is social and economic influences. A number of factors could be discussed under this heading, but the discussion here will be limited to (1) career influence and (2) the supply of and demand for office jobs. Career influence is made up of what an employee is looking forward to when he accepts a job and the influence of this ambition on his work. The pay for a job may be too low, in terms of what the job requires; but because of career influence, the employee willingly forgoes the higher and appropriate pay in order to get ultimately to a job he wants. The case of a young law graduate in a law office illustrates this point. On the other hand, the career influence may cause a job to be rated too highly by the employee, based on the actual job requirements. The job might be of the dead-end type and offer no usable training or advancement beyond a well-known level. In this case, sufficient salary must be paid to secure and hold the proper type of employee.

For the most part, salary rates are affected by the condition of supply and demand. These economic factors are dynamic; they change with time and exert a "push and pull" effect on salary rates. As a matter of practical consideration, recognition must be given to significant changes in the supply and demand for employees of specific skills. *Temporarily,* minor adjustments might have to be made in order to alleviate serious labor shortage difficulties. For example, current conditions may make it necessary to start a new employee at a figure higher than the usual starting wage but still within the range of the job. Or in unusual cases, the rate may be outside the job range; but such a condition usually does not last and might be viewed as an emergency case. If it does persist, however, it is well to revalue the job and change the classification, thus giving reality to the salary administration plan.

This does not mean that the salary ranges established primarily through job evaluation should be ignored whenever the labor market is either generally tight or loose. It does mean some deviation for some jobs —generally very few—which have become out of line because of the effect of current economic forces. As a matter of fact, the job-evaluating factors, such as education, experience, and responsibility, are themselves functions of time and of the economic forces of supply and demand. It is therefore reasonable to expect some minor adjustments in salary rates as a result of the influence of supply and demand for employees of specific office skills.

CHAPTER SEVEN

DEVELOPING OFFICE EMPLOYEES

Only the individual can make himself a better manager.
The company and the boss can help. But in the long run
all personal development is just that—personal.
—Richard S. Reynolds, Jr.

THE PLANNED development of employees is the goal of formal employee training efforts. It is vital in managerial actuating and has grown tremendously during recent years. Employee training is an everyday activity in most enterprises. Employees acquire their training either by means of planned and well-administered programs or by a hit-or-miss method which includes learning by mistakes, by trial and error, and by absorption. Since training is vital and goes on continually, progressive managers have set up definite training programs so that proper direction and control can be given to make the employee's work contribution more useful to the enterprise.

FUNDAMENTALS OF DEVELOPING

Most employees are developing most of the time through the acquisition of additional knowledge and skill. This is a perfectly natural process. The sources include personal performance, behavior of other employees, hearing, observing, and imitating. These means are commonly referred to as "experience." Development from these sources places a strong emphasis on what is practical and is conditioned extensively by experiment and accident. As such, it is neither an efficient means nor necessarily applicable to the employee's job.

Intentional efforts to teach someone can be far more effective, provided the efforts are properly managed. Beginning with what the trainee now knows and can perform, it is possible to determine what the trainee must know and be able to do in order to perform successfully particular work assignments. The differential between what is now known and what is needed constitutes the gap which training seeks to fill. This gap is reduced gradually, because learning is a gradual process. An employee learns bit by bit, not all at once. Knowing the gap to be filled and considering the gradual doses which can be absorbed by the trainee and in what sequence, the formal training operation can be set in motion. Usually, tie-ins or association of new concepts with knowledge or skills already possessed by the trainee proves effective in training work.

There exist today many different schools of thought about the means of training. However, the objective should be foremost in determining the form of training to provide. Fundamentally, all instruction should (1)

---

1. A person learns best what he likes best.
2. A person learns by doing; watching or listening is insufficient.
3. A person remembers longer if he understands the *why* of the knowledge.
4. A person tries harder for rewards than he does to avoid punishments.
5. A person learns fastest when the teaching makes it easier for the learner to learn.

FIG. 25.   Some key points in learning.

proceed from the known to the unknown, (2) go from the simple to the complex, and (3) follow the order of "prepare, present, and apply."

There exist today many different schools of thought about the means of training. However, the objective should be foremost in determining the form of training to provide. Fundamentally, all instruction should (1) proceed from the known to the unknown, (2) go from the simple to the complex, and (3) follow the order of "prepare, present, and apply."

Basic considerations in the activity of acquiring knowledge and skill warrant emphasis in our discussion at this time. Of prime importance is the trainee's personal interest in learning. Economic or social gains may motivate him, but a stimulus must be present. Necessarily, people start from where they are in any training effort, and they are most likely to want to learn when they see what is taught is helpful to them. In addition, the trainee must be in a receptive mood, emotionally settled, and free from worries, personal troubles, and anxieties. Lastly, it must be recognized that the trainee must learn for himself; he must subject himself to the learning process. The instructor's role is primarily one of guidance and stimulation.

Figure 25 lists some key points in learning. Keeping these simple truths in mind will assist anyone who is helping others to develop.

OBJECTIVES OF SUPERVISORY TRAINING

Three basic requirements are common to most successful supervisors: (1) technical proficiency, (2) facility in visualization, and (3) ability in human relations. Under technical skill are included such things as effective application of one's knowledge of specific techniques in handling and processing information, office practices, office layout, and the like. Essentially, technical skill deals with tangible operations and is the most common type of skill possessed.

Facility in visualization means the capacity to picture mentally the managerial operations, to envision their relations, to exercise creativeness, and to evolve means for accomplishing definite goals. It involves intangibles, it includes perception of the management process, and it implies possession of an all-inclusive conceptual viewpoint and understanding about all the elements through which the major tasks will be accomplished. It is especially important for the office supervisor.

Ability in human relations is essential to supervisory ability and growth. Much of the discussion in this section of the book deals with this topic; but for emphasis, it can be repeated that knowledge and skill in human relations deals with manager-nonmanager relationships, the general attitude toward people, the evaluating of human motivations, and the winning of loyalty, support, and willing cooperation.

OBJECTIVES OF EMPLOYEE TRAINING

Comparing respective job requirements to the qualifications of the employee performing the jobs will reveal certain areas in which employee training might prove helpful. Future plans of the office, anticipated increases in personnel, and changes in methods are direct and basic sources for determining the objectives of an employee training program.

Each employee should have complete knowledge of what constitutes his job and what its relationship is to other jobs in the organization. This should not be left to chance. Planned efforts in the form of a training program should be utilized to get job content information to each employee. Improved relations are a certainty when the employee understands completely what his job is, the relationship of his work to other work in the department, and, in time, that of his department to the entire organization structure.

Up-to-date knowledge of operating policies and procedures is another important and common objective in office training. Information on personnel practices should be made known to all. Likewise, the general scope of desired public relations and the quality of paper work required are among the types of information which should be a part of every employee's knowledge.

Each employee should have knowledge of the best known methods of doing his work. It is not sufficient for managers alone to have this knowledge; a manager must see to it that the employees also know, for only then is a satisfactory efficiency in work output possible.

Also, recognition or advancement should be extended when training is completed satisfactorily. This may take the form of improved status, public recognition, increased earnings, or promotion. It is a mistake for an enterprise to develop an employee for a better job or to improve or add to his knowledge and skill without subsequently offering him a job on which he can use the newly acquired ability, either in the present or at some future date, within or outside the enterprise.

ADVANTAGES OF TRAINING

When the above objectives are attained definite advantages accrue. One who really manages makes use of training to help him manage. To the management member, training assists in improving his managerial knowledge and skill. For example, creating effective plans, maintaining proper standards of quality, building a satisfactory organization structure, delegating authority, and stimulating employees are all assisted by effective training.

In addition, the responsibility of supervision is lessened. Training does not eliminate the need for good supervision but it reduces the requirement for detailed and constant supervision. A well-trained office employee is self-reliant in his work, because he knows what to do and how to do it. Under such conditions, close supervision is ordinarily not mandatory.

Also, the best available methods of performing the work can be standardized and made available to all employees. High levels of performance become the rule rather than the exception. The advantages of past knowledge and experience can be retained.

Furthermore, office employees, well trained, will usually show a greater increase in, and a higher quality of, work output than will an untrained group. Employees do a more intelligent job and make fewer mistakes when they possess the know-how, have an understanding of their jobs and of the interdependence of one job and another, and know the *why* of the company's policies and procedures. And it is important to note that morale can be boosted effectively *after* the employee knows what to do.

On the other hand, these advantages are not obtained without a price. Certain difficulties and possible losses are incurred and should be recognized in any training program. First of all, regular office work is likely to be interrupted or delayed by time spent in training. The output of the trainee might be temporarily reduced. Also, training might foster dependence upon others for solutions to challenges which the employee should think through for himself. Self-reliance and capacity for new ideas might be stifled. Furthermore, competent training leaders are difficult to obtain. When mediocre instruction is utilized, not only may the results of the training be below what is expected, but they may actually prove harmful.

TYPES OF TRAINING

Training can be classified in many ways. One useful classification is training for present jobs and training for future jobs. Another is training for any or all of the following: job knowledge, job skills, and attitudes. Still another is training for basic information, for personal development, and for specific production in definite work application. A useful list showing the range and types of training may be outlined as follows:

1. *Preemployment Training.* This deals with the type and amount of instruction needed by inexperienced employees prior to their entering the office. This training is generally provided by educational institutions outside the enterprise, such as high schools, universities, business colleges, night schools, and correspondence courses. Preemployment training is generally broader and more fundamental than the other types of training. It is intended to provide basic skills. Likewise, it sometimes is of a theoretical nature, in contrast to the practical aspect of the other types; it seeks to provide an intellectual background and to develop the art of thinking and reasoning.

2. *Induction Training.* The objective of induction training is to provide the new employee with the information necessary for a complete knowledge and understanding of practices and procedures of the enterprise. Included in this aspect of training are welcoming the new employee to the company, explaining the office rules and regulations, acquainting him with employees' benefits, informing him of the company's policies and operations, and telling him what is expected of him as an employee. The new office employee's impression of the company is frequently formed during the first several hours at the new job. Introductions should be made to the new employee's department head, fellow employees, and those supervisors with whom he will be associated. If it is possible, an introduction to one of the officers is also helpful, as this gives the new employee a feeling of worth and helps him to visualize the extent of the company. Experience shows it is a good idea to give the employee some

job which he can do without too much instruction and then leave him by himself. This gives the new employee a chance to digest some of the new surroundings. Follow this up with contacts about every hour or so throughout the rest of the day. Encourage the new employee to ask questions.

3. *On-the-Job Training.* This type of training aims to give the employee the necessary skill required for a specific job. It seeks to fill the gap between the ability the worker can supply and the ability the job requires. The job can be either that of the present or some future assignment. In some cases, the job is of a higher grade than the

TYPES OF TRAINING GIVEN TO VARIOUS CLASSIFICATIONS OF EMPLOYEES

Classification of Employee	Type of Training	Training Required
New	Induction	To give information relative to the job and to the policies and practices of the company.
	On-the-job	Specific training in the important details of the employee's job. To help the employee acquire the necessary knowledge and skill.
Seasoned	On-the-job	To instruct in changes in procedures, routines, policies, and new equipment. Also, to prepare for jobs of higher grade (promotion).
Transferred	Induction	To give information relative to new duties and work environment.
	On-the-job	Specific training in the important details of the new job. To help the employee acquire the necessary knowledge and skill.
Supervisor	Supervisory	To give information relative to the theory and practical application of supervisory techniques.

FIG. 26.

employee's present one; in other words, the employee is being prepared for promotion. The makeup of on-the-job training takes many different forms, including lectures in specific subjects, practice on new machines, job rotation—including all jobs of a certain group, special assignments of a temporary nature, understudying a junior executive, special courses, reading assignments, and special workshops by professional associations. On-the-job training stresses just that—on the job—but some of the training may be acquired, in part, outside the enterprise. The entire program, however, should be carefully coordinated.

4. *Supervisory Training*. One of the most important types of training in any enterprise is supervisory training. Training of supervisors is vital because of their essentiality in management. Special courses in supervisory training have been designed, and many of these are generally considered effective. Discussion of supervisory training is included in the chapter on office supervision (Chapter 4).

Figure 26 indicates the type of training which is given to employees of different classifications or circumstances. For example, the new employee is given induction training and on-the-job training. The former provides information relative to his new job and to the policies and practices of the company; the latter includes specific training to help him acquire necessary skill.

MAKEUP OF TRAINING PROGRAM

In addition to ample consideration for the fundamentals of training, the objectives sought, and the types of training available, the makeup of any training program should devote sufficient thought to (1) the trainees, (2) the instructor, (3) the training period, (4) the training material, and (5) the training methods.

1. *Trainees*. Proper selection of trainees is of major importance if permanent, gainful results are to be obtained. A trainee should be trained for the kind of job he likes and is fitted to perform. In this respect, training is closely related to the selection of personnel. Evidence is quite conclusive that careful screening of candidates for training raises the effectiveness of the training work.

In the case of supervisory training, it is best to include all supervisors and those considered for promotion to such posts. Excluding some employees on the basis that they do not need the training or that they are already doing their work satisfactorily is a poor policy. Even outstanding supervisors profit from well-managed training programs, and their presence assists in many ways the less competent supervisors in attendance.

2. *Instructor*. A key figure in a good training program is the instructor, as a capable teacher contributes immeasurably to its success. Qualified instructors may be obtained from inside or outside the company; however, many office employees are not good teachers. The efficient employee does not necessarily have the ability to teach. Instructors need many qualifications besides knowing how to do the work. A good teacher has the skill to instruct and is tolerant, understanding, and patient. Also important is an appreciation for the value of the training work in relation to the enterprise and an understanding of what the employee goes through

in order to acquire the skill and knowledge which the program is designed to achieve.

3. *Training Period.*   The length of the training period depends upon the skill to be acquired, the trainee's learning capacity, and the training media used. For example, a simple indoctrination program for clerks may require an hour a day over a period of a week, while a course in accounting machines may be given two hours a week for 15 weeks. The use of effective visual material usually helps to reduce the training time. Some training directors claim that effective visualization reduces the teaching time by upward of 35 percent. Also, certain means of training such as programmed instruction, discussed below, which is of a visual nature, is reputed to save up to 70 percent of training time.

To maintain interest and to secure maximum accomplishment, no single session should last longer than two hours. One hour is even better. The best practice is to pay employees for training time if the course relates in any way to their work. Many states have laws or rulings affecting training time; and in addition, certain federal laws are applicable. Controversial issues are likely to appear if the employee does any productive work during the training time, if the training is outside regular working hours, of if the training work is intended to train the employee for a new or additional skill. It is advisable to check federal and prevailing state laws to help determine whether trainee or company time should be used.

4. *Training Material.*   A text or some written material is usually desirable as a basis for instruction, review, and reference. For most subjects, a satisfactory book can be selected; but in instances where the course content is of a special nature, it may be well to prepare material for this specific use. A complete outline of the entire course should be made with the main topics included under each meeting or session. When a text is used, the parts to be covered must be clearly indicated; and assignments which require some preparatory time should be made for every meeting. This helps to keep the program on schedule, points the meeting toward definite subjects, and usually assists in the progress and satisfaction of the trainee.

5. *Training Methods.*   There exist many different office training methods. For convenience, we will confine this discussion to the following 12 different methods, listed alphabetically: coaching and counseling, computer assisted instruction, conferences, demonstrations, guided experience, in-basket technique, job rotation, lectures, problem solving, programmed instruction, role playing, and understudy method. Choice of office training method depends upon many factors, including the objectives of the training, the number of trainees, the preferences of the

instructor, the type of material to be covered, the cost, the time allotted, and the wishes of the trainees.

Coaching and counseling are discussed in Chapter 4, but a few more words will be stated here to emphasize their importance in training efforts. These media are normally work-centered and fact-centered individual efforts aimed to convey useful work information and to improve skill. Coaching emphasizes "setting up the plays," but permitting the employee to carry them out as best he can. Motivation and practical instruction are essential. The instructor must have the respect of the trainee, understand how he feels, and possess an ability to use analogies and demonstrations. Counseling stresses assisting an employee to recognize his strengths and weaknesses in fulfilling the requirements of his job. The counselor spends most of his time listening. His role is to help the trainee help himself, to become independent in his own right, and to build confidence in himself. The amount of direction and assistance given depends upon the individual being counseled. Both coaching and counseling emphasize a person-to-person individualized relationship. Essentially, it is an informal rather than a formal method of training.

The computer assisted instruction (CAI) is one of the newer means of instruction. The trainee takes a course by means of a computerized teaching machine. Instructions, questions, and guidance are stored in the computer and presented to the trainee by means of a typewriterlike communications terminal linked to the computer. Up to 12 trainees can hook into the course at the same time. After giving an identification number to verify trainee and course, the first question is written out by the computer on a continuous paper form of the terminal unit. In a course on statistics, for example, the first question might be, "How is the arithmetic average calculated? Type answer." If you answer, "By determining the number in the series appearing most frequently," the computer will answer immediately, "That answer is incorrect. The arithmetical average is not determined by the frequency of a number in the series but by averaging mathematically. Will you answer again?" Prompted by the hint, you now type the answer, "Add the numbers of the series and divide this sum by the quantity of numbers in the series." To this the computer will answer, "Correct," then proceed to the next question. To date, CAI appears to work best in conjunction with a human teacher who can answer questions and conduct periodic seminars. Computer trainees retain more material than conventional trainees and in a test of a statistics course needed only 13 hours to complete what requires 45 hours in an ordinary classroom.

The conference method permits trainees to express themselves orally and to exchange thoughts, and enables the instructor to judge the trainee's

understanding of the subject material. The conference method is especially popular in supervisory training. Trainees are encouraged to express
themselves freely. A group of about 20 participants is the ideal size for
best results from the conference method. Demonstrations provide forceful
presentation of how the job is done. This means stresses learning by eye
rather than by ear and is especially helpful for jobs where physical skills
are vital. The guided experience method utilizes evaluation of the trainee
to reveal his weaknesses; then, the causes of these weaknesses are
decided, and experience to remedy them is planned. Extreme care is taken
to select the proper work assignments so that the trainee's shortcomings
are ultimately removed. The assignments vary and include such things as
writing reports, serving on committees, solving specific problems, performing research work, and working on normal day-to-day tasks. Like
coaching and counseling, the guided experience method can be considered
a highly personalized, informal type of training.

The in-basket technique realistically simulates actual office conditions.
Actually it is in the nature of a business game. From two to about fifteen
play the game which ordinarily takes two hours—one hour actual playing
time and one hour of discussion among the players following conclusion of
the game. Each trainee or player sits at a desk on which there is an "in"
and an "out" basket, paper, and pencil. Instructions are given by the
instructor indicating, for example, that you have certain helpers and you
are leaving on your three-week vacation tomorrow. Identical packets of
papers are then placed in the "in" baskets of all players. These papers
require your office managerial attention. A typical packet may contain
three letters, five memos, a telegram, two reports, and four telephone
messages. Each trainee studies the materials and writes what he believes
is the most appropriate action, clips the material to the original paper,
and places it in his "out" basket. Figure 27 shows a representative paper
with answer written at the bottom. The in-basket technique is reasonable
in cost, highly practical, and can include an almost unlimited number of
potential problems and situations.

Job rotation, sometimes referred to as the "merry-go-round" basis,
rotates trainees among different organizational units, thus providing the
trainees with overall knowledge of the company's operations and the work
done by each unit, and the opportunity to participate in the affairs of the
various units. This method assists the individual to think in terms of
universal managerial principles rather than the immediate activities at
hand. Lectures are effective for initially explaining information to
trainees. They should be carefully prepared, reinforced by the use of
charts, sketches, and models, and presented by a qualified speaker. The
means of problem solving is effective when the problems are well selected

---

June 17, 196-

To: William Danzek

From: Horace Goulet

Subject: Edith Davis

    I understand through informal sources that Edith Davis is dissatisfied with her salary and is looking for another job. To the best of my knowledge she does not have any other job offer at this time. You know, of course, that she is one of the best girls we have had on the job of filing computer data runs and she is extremely capable and efficient in her work. I believe she would be hard to replace especially at her present salary. Within the next few days, I would like to discuss with you a salary increase for Miss Davis even though regular salary reviews are not scheduled at this time.

6/18

Horace:

O.K. to get together on this next thursday at 3 P.M. Please review our entire work history with Edith Davis and find out if present salary is real cause for dissatisfaction. Also check Personnel to see if any likely applicants for this filing job are on file.

W. D.

FIG. 27. Typical paper from an "in-basket" training session. The top portion poses the problem, the bottom portion is the respondent's answer.

and bring out considerations pertinent to the work at hand. In short, solving the problems should meet specific development needs, such as an ability to analyze and relate given facts, to determine the problem to be solved, to read and to substantiate the recommended actions to be taken. Unless a developmental need is met, this method of training may be inadequate, time-consuming, and ineffective.

Programmed instruction is self-instruction and utilizes a systematic method of presenting information to the trainee. Presented one step or frame at a time, the material can be easily understood and absorbed. The increasing difficulty between two subsequent frames is narrow so that advancement is gradual but continuous and complex material is encountered only by the trainee prepared for it. The trainee advances at his own individual pace and learns at the speed most convenient for him. For each frame, he is required to select an answer from several alternatives and checks his answer with the approved reply. Thus immediate feedback is provided. He proceeds only after knowing the correct response to the question of the immediate frame. Programmed instruction incorporates sound instructional principles in that the trainee is actively participating in the teaching-learning process, the material is presented to lead each trainee into making the correct response, uniformity and consistency of instruction are possible, and the trainee advances gradually from the simple to the complex aspects of the material. Various research studies reveal the effectiveness of programmed instruction. To illustrate, in imparting knowledge of how to operate a modern office machine, training time required 31 percent less time with the trainees retaining 53 percent more knowledge compared to that obtained with conventional methods. Furthermore, programmed instruction permits training on a decentralized basis, is suited for individual training—a group is not needed, and the instructor can concentrate on special problems of training; he need not spend the majority of his time on routine training work.

Role playing narrows the gap between talking about what should be done and actually doing it. For training purposes, the playing out of a typical problem situation can be quite effective. It is especially helpful in situations involving employee relations. The method permits the trainees to participate, to gain an insight into their own behavior, and to look at the problem from many different viewpoints. By means of the understudy method, the trainee works as an assistant or helper to his teacher, thus acquiring familiarity with the work and practices of his teacher, who normally is an employee at the same or higher organizational level as the trainee. Experience with dynamic events and acquaintance with the atmosphere and position in which the trainee will eventually perform are acquired. On major issues, the trainee may be required to submit complete data affecting the issue along with his recommendations for action. In this way, thinking is stimulated, and the accepting of responsibility is encouraged. The understudy method is commonly used in supervisory training.

COST OF TRAINING

Training costs money. Many analyses of its cost are unrealistic, in that comparisons are made between the expenditures of "no training"—actually a misleading term—and those of a formal training program. The fact is that training costs are tangible and intangible. Erroneously, the latter group is commonly ignored in the cost of training.

Under tangible training costs are training materials, nonproductive time of trainee, and nonproductive time of employee instructor, or fee charged, if an outsider. Under the intangible classification are such things as a longer time for the trainee to attain a reasonable level of production, loss of employees seeking better job opportunities, time of experienced employees asked to "show me how to do this" by the trainee, loss due to work spoilage and errors, practicing of poor work methods, and improper work viewpoints and attitudes being permitted to develop and spread.

Training is a necessity in modern management, and reasonable expenditures for it should be made. The amount depends upon the needs and the aims of the office. However, costs should be kept under control. Management members should have some idea of what is being accomplished for the expenditures being made. This brings up the question of training effectiveness.

EFFECTIVENESS OF TRAINING

From the managerial viewpoint, it is an excellent idea to measure the effectiveness of training efforts. The evaluation, however, must be in terms of a particular training problem. This problem may be expressed in the form of questions, such as:

1. Has the training increased production?
2. Has there been a decrease in the number of errors?
3. Has there been a reduction in labor turnover?
4. Has there been a reduction in absenteeism, requests for transfers, and number of grievances?
5. Has the attitude, work environment, and enthusiasm of the office work force improved?

It is usually best to measure effectiveness by departments or by some homogeneous group, for the problems of measurement become quite complex when the entire office is considered. It is advisable to make comparisons between office groups as units. A good procedure is to use as a control one group which is characterized by little or no formal training, by training of a particular type, or by a different method of training. Special care should be exercised to see that the groups compared are reasonably similar with respect to such factors as age, sex, and time of week, month, or year.

Evaluating the results of training is not, however, a simple matter. Many companies make little effort to evaluate training results as such, or they are satisfied with general overall indications of the training's worth. It is difficult to determine what factors contribute to employee development.

It is possible to overdo training to the point that the efforts and costs in its behalf exceed the highest estimates of benefits within a reasonable period. Training should be carefully managed; it should not be engaged in simply because "it is the thing to do." It is a continuous, not an "off and on," activity. It can start on a small scale and subsequently increase as the benefits become known and the needs and progress of the enterprise dictate.

As a guide, these points should be kept in mind: (1) Office training is desirable and necessary and is performed regardless of whether a formal program is carried on or not; (2) office training must be tailor-made to fit the specific need of the enterprise; (3) the questions of *what* training should be conducted, and *when, where,* and *how,* require answering; (4) office training should be based on the needs of the office as shown by job analysis, prevalence of errors, low work output, employees' attitudes, and supervisory effectiveness; (5) office training should be preceded by careful selection of trainees; and (6) the training of office supervisors is vital.

CHAPTER EIGHT

OFFICE SAFETY AND

TRADE UNIONS

*Underlying practically all our attempts to bring agreement
is the assumption that agreement is brought about by
changing people's minds—other people's.*
—S. I. Hayakawa

PROVIDING a safe place in which to work and an orderly process mutually evolved for determining the general conditions under which the work will be done are major attributes in actuating employees. In this chapter we will discuss first the subject of office safety. Following this the main highlights of office trade unionism will be presented.

OFFICE ACCIDENT OCCURRENCE

Accidents can and do happen to office employees; they enjoy no automatic exemption. These accidents come about in a number of ways. For example, some cleaning fluids used on office machines are inflammable, and cases are on record where the fumes from the cleaning fluid were ignited by a spark from the electric motor of the machine, resulting in a flash fire which caused severe burns to office employees. Severe falls and injuries result from slipping on highly polished floors and running on stairways by women in high-heeled shoes. Reclining too far back in a chair can result in the occupant's being thrown with considerable force; and serious, sometimes permanent, injuries have been suffered by office employees in this way.

There is a cause for every accident. It is some defect or lack of action which must be corrected in order to prevent a recurrence of the accident. Falling down a stairway is not a cause; it is a result—an accident. The causes may be loose papers on the stair treads, inadequate lighting on the

117

stairway, or the employee's failure to watch where he is stepping. These conditions must be rectified in order to achieve better safety results.

Some writers have classified the causes of accidents under three headings: mechanical, physiological, and psychological. These terms are self-explanatory. Under mechanical causes, for example, are classified such things as improper lighting, unguarded machines, and technical defects in equipment. Physiological causes include bad eyesight and age of employees; psychological causes cover such things as the employee's

Courtesy: "GM Folks," General Motors Corp., Detroit

FIG. 28.   The practices illustrated commonly result in accidents. These pictures were especially posed for accident prevention promotional work.

tendency to take unnecessary chances, carelessness, horseplay, and temporary emotional and mental disturbances. These causes are interrelated and must be attacked jointly in most practical activities designed to reduce accidents. Figure 28 illustrates practices that frequently result in accidents.

MANAGERIAL SAFETY ACTION

Experience and records show that accidents can be reduced; in fact, most can be prevented entirely. The best course of action for preventing accidents depends upon the circumstances in each particular case. Some advocate the so-called triple E program, which consists of engineering, education, and enforcement. That is, the first step is to engineer all equipment and machines with safety guards, cutoff switches, and other devices to make them as safe as is technically possible. Next, education for all employees is provided, to instill work habits and practices for winning high safety achievements. Last, enforcement insures that safety regulations are carried out.

This means that the initiative rests with the manager, but he must win the cooperation of the employee to make office safety really effective. Aggressive managerial action is required. Merely supplying a safe working place is insufficient. The manager must also see to it that safety measures are recognized and enforced; but what is more important, he must accomplish this with enthusiastic approval and encouragement by the nonmanagement members.

INITIAL SAFETY STEPS TO BE TAKEN

Hazards causing accidents must be identified before they can be eliminated. Available safety information reveals that the main types of office accidents have to do with slipping, tripping, handling materials, being hit by falling objects, and striking against objects. Among the more common hazards which result in office accidents are:

Defective electric cords lying across aisles, and loose connections
Paper clips and thumbtacks on the floor
Loose linoleum or carpeting
Slippery floors
Open desk drawer or file drawer
Tilting backward too far in office chair
Sharp burrs on edges of metal office equipment
Sharp pointed pencils placed in upright position in handkerchief coat pocket
Broken glass desk top
Exposed moving parts of office machines
Splinters and loose veneer on wood desks and chairs
Bottles, papers, or books stacked on top of filing cabinets
Protruding pencil sharpeners and power and telephone outlets
Reading while walking
Running in aisle, on stairways, or through doorways

Assistance in locating hazards to eliminate is provided by a check list such as that shown in Figure 29. In addition, an analysis of the accident reports can help in locating areas that need attention.

With factual data as a background, steps can be taken to incorporate

OFFICE SAFETY INSPECTION DATA

Carefully inspect the office, and for each question, check whether a hazard exists. If "Yes," briefly note the important details.

QUESTION	DOES HAZARD EXIST?		COMMENTS (GIVE LOCATION AND DETAILS.)
	Yes	No	
1. Are aisles obstructed?			
2. Do pencil sharpeners project over desk or table?			
3. Are file drawers kept closed when not in use?			
4. Are machines properly guarded?			
5. Are glass desk tops broken?			
6. Are there any sharp metal projections on any equipment?			
7. Is electrical wiring concealed?			
8. Are office accessories insecurely placed?			
9. Are papers and waste properly disposed of?			
10. Are facilities for smokers adequate?			
11. Are materials stacked on desks or cabinets?			
12. Are extension cords used extensively?			
13. Are floors too highly polished?			
14. Is carpeting loose or worn?			

FIG. 29.   Portion of a form designed to assist in determining safety hazards.

needed safety actions into a program. Usually included are the following:

1. *Educate employees to possible dangers.*   Each employee should be made thoroughly aware of all the possible dangers of his job. All the details that make for safety should be carefully explained. These efforts can be planned and made a regular part of the job process and the training work. In this manner, the correct way of doing the job, which is also the safe way, becomes habitual. Safety is built right into the job—it is a part of the job.

2. *Provide safe work areas.*   Supplying all the necessary provisions for safe working places and equipment for employees is paramount. Office floors should be covered with nonslippery material; adequate lighting should be provided; desks and chairs should be free of sharp edges.

3. *Promote first-aid service.*   Insistence upon first-aid treatment for minor injuries means little if adequate facilities are not available. When these facilities are provided, managers show that they wish all injured employees to receive treatment promptly.

4. *Make safety clothing available.* The use of special clothing designed to protect employees from injuries should also be included. Plastic aprons, for example, should be available to employees working around large quantities of ink, glue, and cleaning solutions. Likewise, finger guards should be provided to employees doing work where the chances of suffering paper cuts are quite high.

5. *Maintain good housekeeping practices.* Good housekeeping in the office is essential for good safety work. The habits of orderliness and cleanliness contribute to good office safety because they help to set good examples for employees and to keep the office personnel safety-minded. Stairways should be kept clear of all loose objects; aisles should be marked for traffic lanes; an adequate number of wastepaper baskets should be furnished; and regular cleanup service should be provided.

OFFICE SAFETY RECORDS

Effective accident prevention work requires that adequate records be kept of all accidents. It is important to know what accidents happened, where, when, the types of injuries incurred, and the conditions which caused them. By studying such data, a manager is able to take intelligent corrective action and knows where to stress safety efforts.

There are two widely used and accepted indexes in safety statistics: (1) the frequency rate and (2) the severity rate. These names are self-explanatory: The frequency rate measures the occurrence of accidents, and the severity rate measures the seriousness of accidents. The indexes are used to show the relative values and trends within any group and the comparisons among different groups.

1. *Frequency rate.* The frequency rate can be defined as the number of disabling injuries suffered per million man-hours worked. The formula is:

$$\text{Frequency rate} = \frac{\text{Number of disabling injuries} \times 1,000,000}{\text{Total number of man-hours worked}}$$

Disabling injuries are frequently referred to as "lost-time accidents arising out of and in the course of employment." The National Safety Council classifies the following types of injuries as disabling injuries:

a) Death.

b) Permanent total disability. Any injury or combination of injuries suffered in one accident which permanently and totally incapacitates an employee from following any gainful occupation. Loss of both eyes or of both hands is an example.

c) Permanent partial disability. Any injury suffered in one accident which results in the loss of any member or part of a member of the body but which does not result in death or permanent total disability.

d) Temporary total disability. Any injury suffered in one accident which results in no permanent injury but which prevents the injured person from returning to a regularly established job within 24 hours after the start of the shift during which he was injured.

The total number of man-hours is best obtained from payroll records or time cards. If these are unavailable, the number can be estimated by multiplying the average number of employees by the average number of hours worked during the period considered.

2. *Severity rate.* The severity rate is the number of days charged as a result of injuries per million man-hours worked. The formula is:

$$\text{Severity rate} = \frac{\text{Time charged (in days)} \times 1{,}000{,}000}{\text{Total number of man-hours worked}}$$

Days charged are sometimes called "days of disability." However, the time charged away from the job does not accurately measure the severity of the accident. Therefore, tables have been set up indicating an arbitrary number of days which should be used for various types of accidents. For example, an accident resulting in death or in permanent total disability is charged at the rate of 6,000 days for each case. This is approximately 20 years. A permanent partial disability resulting in the loss of a hand is charged at 3,000 days.

Available safety data show that the office frequency rates and severity rates are among the lowest of any industry classification. This is shown in Figure 30. It is encouraging to note that with several exceptions, the rates are declining for every industry—safety is progressing.

Records on accident costs are also helpful in improving safety accomplishments inasmuch as the amount of expenditure has some relationship to the efforts directed to this area. Budgets of these costs are desirable, and actions to get the most benefits for a given expenditure should be encouraged.

It is a well-known fact that accidents are expensive. The loss might be in money, skill, time, human suffering, work output, or interruption in the flow of work. The hidden or incidental costs of accidents are much greater than the measurable direct costs. Such things as the cost of hiring and training new employees, the interference with production, and the loss of good will are sizable expenses not generally though of in connection with the costs of accidents. The ratio of hidden to direct costs of accidents may

THREE-YEAR FREQUENCY AND SEVERITY RATES OF SELECTED INDUSTRIES

INDUSTRY	FREQUENCY RATES					SEVERITY RATES				
	1958–60	1959–61	1960–62	1961–63	1962–64	1958–60	1959–61	1960–62	1961–63	1962–64
Offices..............	0.65	0.69	0.68	0.76	0.71	115	158	117	127	130
Automobile..........	2.34	2.13	1.91	1.73	1.77	258	249	228	215	207
Chemical.............	3.54	3.44	3.42	3.30	3.25	528	476	489	419	395
Construction..........	17.97	18.70	19.07	19.08	19.08	2,350	2,247	2,296	2,376	2,498
Lumbering............	23.82	23.64	20.43	18.40	17.37	2,375	2,166	1,760	1,596	1,642
Printing and Publishing.	6.66	6.92	7.07	6.81	7.48	369	338	313	258	411
Steel................	3.29	3.30	3.25	3.31	3.34	794	796	739	713	695
Tobacco.............	6.65	6.48	6.06	5.88	5.78	307	266	332	399	440

Compiled from National Safety Council, Inc., "Accident Facts" (Chicago, 1961–65)

FIG. 30. Comparison of safety statistics.

be as high as 4 to 1, which means that total accident costs are far greater than most people realize.

OFFICE SAFETY PERSONNEL

It is important that there be a recognized head of office safety work. This person should be given complete responsibility for the direction and guidance of all office safety efforts. The person in charge might be the office manager himself, or the office manager might appoint a subordinate to the job. Generally, the safety director need not spend all of his time on safety, but it is advisable for him to devote a certain amount of time regularly to the program.

Department heads are the key personnel in accident prevention work. In many respects, the success of the entire safety program depends upon the supervisors. It is promoted by the cooperation of the department heads, and they can do more than anyone else toward keeping the employees safety-minded. Furthermore, supervisors can correct unsafe conditions, they can see that safety rules are followed, that first aid is provided in case of accident, and that proper reports are filled out.

Because participation promotes acceptance, the use of a safety committee with rotating membership is recommended. A five-member committee, with membership rotating bimonthly, usually works out very well. The system of replacements should be such that not more than two new members are added at any one time, thus insuring that the remaining three members are familiar with the work of the committee. The work of this group is advisory. It submits suggestions for the reduction of accidents within the office. Frequently, the safety committee may also:

1. Sponsor accident prevention contests.
2. Review safety suggestions made by the employees.
3. Make regular safety inspections of the office.
4. Suggest additions and changes in safety rules.
5. Post safety materials on the bulletin boards.
6. Maintain the first-aid equipment.

PROMOTING SAFETY CONSCIOUSNESS

The mental attitude of the employee toward safety is exceedingly important in accident prevention work. There is a great deal of truth in the saying: "The best safety device in all the world is located an inch or two above the eyebrows." The employee who "thinks safety" and who has developed a safety consciousness "from the ears up" has gone a long way toward preventing accidents.

All efforts designed to keep safety on the employee's mind and to keep accident prevention a live subject in the office will help substantially in the safety program. Although it may seem strange, it is a common occurrence for people to be careless. Safety-mindedness requires alert-mindedness. Safety work is a continuous process, requiring constant reminders to the employee to work safely, to avoid taking chances, and to keep safety foremost in his thoughts. The task is not an easy one, but persistence and steadfastness of purpose will achieve good results.

It is a truism that for the most part, people attach the same degree of importance to activities as do their leaders. If the managers believe in, and are actively engaged in, accident prevention work, then this same spirit will be picked up by the employees. The safety example set by managers is important in attaining a good safety record.

In addition, safety rules should be explained, and the reasons for their rigid enforcement given to the employees. The entire safety program can be seriously handicapped if there is any letdown in either the education or the enforcement of safety rules. Quite often, having the rules in writing is helpful.

Also, employees should be informed of safety fundamentals. This can take various forms, including articles in company papers, talks at meetings, informal suggestions to employees, movies, and safety instruction cards. This latter medium provides the employee with pertinent suggestions about safety and serves as a series of timely reminders, helping to keep safety on the minds of the employees. Figure 31 shows several examples of safety instruction cards.

Pictures, posters, and cartoon sketches can also be used to arouse the employee's interest in safety. It is usually best to have this material specific in nature, telling the employee what to do under particular conditions. Giving the employee general safety cautions and slogans is probably of limited value. It is usually well to supplement this type of safety promotion with intensive individual follow-up. The bulletin boards used should be located in areas that are frequently seen, accessible, and in full view.

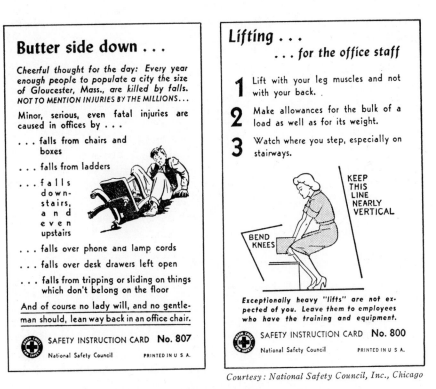

Courtesy: National Safety Council, Inc., Chicago

FIG. 31.   Safety instruction cards.

Lastly, safety contests are helpful. They stress the competitive spirit and usually rely upon the employee's desire to excel. An award in the form of a plaque, banner, special pin, or money may be given the individual, group, or department having the best safety record for a given period. A reversal of this technique can also be used, and it is generally effective. In this case, a booby prize is given the unit having the poorest safety record, with the requirement that this "award" be displayed prominently. This approach appeals to the employee's pride and to his desire to escape any designation which makes him look ridiculous. Like all promotional plans, safety contests must be publicized and made acceptable to the employees.

THE OFFICE AND TRADE UNIONS

Trade unions for office employees have existed for a number of years. Among the oldest are the editorial employees of some newspapers, organized around 1890; the National Association of Letter Carriers, created in 1892; and the Brotherhood of Railway and Steamship Clerks, organized in 1899. These early unions were loosely organized, judged in terms of present-day standards.

During the following several decades, other office unions came into being, among which are the following: the National Federation of Post Office Clerks (organized in 1906), the American Federation of Teachers (1916), the National Federation of Federal Employees (1917), and the American Federation of Governmental Employees (1932). With time additional office unions were formed. Today, there are several hundred strong office unions within the United States. Estimates vary as to their total membership, but it is probably close to 10 percent of the total number of office employees. This may appear minor, but it is a composite figure of all office employees; and in certain enterprises, the extent of office unionization assumes a prominent position.

MANAGEMENT–TRADE-UNION RELATIONS

When a union exists in an office, managers are required to bargain with the authorized representatives concerning "wages and other conditions of employment." In other words, a process which might be called "collective cooperation" is used, whereby employers and representatives of employees arrive at agreements covering compensation and the conditions under which employees will work. This usually means that policies concerning matters such as wages, discharge, discipline, and transfer must be discussed with the union representatives and incorporated into a mutually agreed upon labor contract. Subsequently, decisions utilizing these policies are made by management members but are frequently subject to question by and explanation to the union, via an established grievance procedure. In essence, the union wants to be consulted and to present its views in matters affecting its members during the decision-making process so that the decision reached will be in keeping with its views. The ultimate decision, however, is made by a management member; but from the practical viewpoint, the decision must be acceptable to the representatives of the employees in order to be entirely effective.

WHY OFFICE EMPLOYEES JOIN OR DO NOT JOIN UNIONS

The growth in office unionization has been slow. Various surveys reveal that office employees do not join a union for these major reasons:

1. *Possible loss of social status and prestige.* Identification of office employees is with "those in the know." The typical office employee works in street clothes; he is around, sees, and sometimes meets the executives of the company. He believes his work is of a high type, is dignified, and has prestige. Frequently, it is looked up to.

2. *Receiving certain benefits of unionism without being members.* In many instances, the benefits negotiated by unions of nonoffice employees are passed along to the office employees of that enterprise. This practice has been termed "a free ride" for the office employees. The practice may be questioned, but it does exist.

3. *Satisfactory working conditions.* Most office employees feel that they work in an area which is cleaner and quieter than that in which many other employees work. Also, they may consider the work safer and not as physically tiring.

4. *The basic characteristics of most office employees.* They are conservative and inclined to stay with the old rather than to try out the new. In addition, about two-thirds of the office employees are women, many of whom are interested in working in offices for only a limited period of time.

In contrast, what is the answer to "Why do office employees join unions"? Among the various reasons, these appear most prominent:

1. *Discontent with present earnings.* Especially is this true when comparisons with wages of factory employees are easily made and the differential between the two are great. Among the greatest contributors to this discontent are slower rates of wage increases for office compared to factory employees, shrinking advantage in fringe benefits enjoyed by office employees, and wage raises for lower-class office jobs without comparable wage adjustments in middle and top office job classes.

2. *Lack of security.* The wide changes taking place in the office, especially growing automation, add to the office employee's fear of losing his job.

3. *Supervisors who are not well trained or informed.* The employees want better work guidance, communication, and participation in matters that affect them.

4. *Lack of a feeling of justice.* Formalized procedures to permit handling of grievances of office employees or to represent them adequately to management representatives are not provided. The employees believe there is no adequate means for them to get their "gripes" to top managers' attention.

CHARACTERISTICS OF CONTRACTS

The majority of current office-union contracts are tailor-made to suit the special conditions of the individual offices. There is, however, some similarity of contracts, since most of them cover the same subject topics. Most contracts contain clauses covering such matters as recognition of the union, union status, union security, salaries, hours of work, seniority, employment procedures, transfers and dismissals, grievance procedures, penalties, maternity leaves, and severance pay. A discussion of several of these subjects follows.

1. *Union recognition clause.* A "recognition of the union" clause points out that the union named in the contract is fully recognized by the employer; frequently, it also states what jobs and what employees are covered by the contract. Sometimes, a statement is included to the effect that the union will not accept into membership those employees in the excluded groups.

2. *Status of union.* Union status concerns the relationship of members of the union with the company. In general, there are three kinds of union status:

1. *Union shop.* Nonunion members may be hired; but after a certain period, they must, as a requirement of employment, become union members.

2. *"Maintenance of membership" shop.* All employees are not required to join the union, but all present union members must retain membership during the time the contract is in force.

3. *Exclusive bargaining shop.* The union is recognized as the exclusive bargaining agent for all employees, but no employee is compelled to join it or to remain a member.[1]

3. *Wage rates.* Clauses on wage rates frequently include the recognition of job classifications and wage rates for each class. Minimum rates only might be stated. Uniform adjustments, either in amount or in

---

[1] The Labor Management Relations Act of 1947 outlawed in interstate commerce (1) the closed shop—in which the employer agrees to hire only union members, and all employees must continue their good standing in the union during their terms of employment and (2) the preferential shop—in which preference in hiring and in layoff is given union members.

percentage, may be provided; and the effective date of such adjustments may be included.

The following is a typical contractual statement pertaining to wages.

SECTION 2. The wage schedules as set forth in this schedule, attached hereto as Exhibit B and made a part hereof, shall apply and be in effect as of July 1, 1967, and shall remain in effect for the life of this agreement.

SECTION 3. Overtime compensation and deductible time lost shall be computed by dividing the monthly salary by one hundred seventy-three and one third (173⅓) to arrive at an hourly rate to be used for such computations.

4. *Layoffs and seniority.* While most unions favor the governing of layoffs and rehires on seniority, they will grant a statement to the effect that seniority shall govern when the employee involved has the ability to do the work under question. Questions arising in connection with seniority are sometimes clarified by the practice of preclassifying employees either by occupation or by departments or divisions. In this way, employees making up a fairly comparable group are associated together.

To illustrate:

SECTION 3. A reduction in working forces resulting in demotions and layoffs will normally be on a departmental seniority basis except for stenographers and filing clerks, who will be on a company-wide basis.

5. *Penalty clauses.* Penalty provisions provide punishment for members who violate parts of the contract. Penalties might be in the form of reductions in pay, temporary or permanent layoffs, or less severe disciplinary measures, depending upon the nature of the violation.

CONTRACT LIMITATIONS

It is not feasible to write a collective bargaining contract which covers every possible source of difference between the employer and the employee. A brief contract stating the points in simple terms usually is sufficient. Attempts to cover all contingencies in great detail will result in complicating the contract and in making it extremely difficult to interpret. Arguments about language technicalities lead to disputes which usually cause trouble.

There must be a spirit of cooperativeness on the part of both interested parties; they must want the contract to work. When both parties have this attitude, even the skimpy and legally poorly written contract can help to expedite harmonious relations. Without this attitude, the success of a well-written contract can be seriously curtailed.

In many respects, questions involving the legal rights are peripheral quizzes—they do not penetrate to the real core of management-union cooperation. Managerial actions and techniques conducive to production and mutual cooperation are paramount considerations, as well as the union's appreciation of the inherent characteristics and conditions under which the office must operate. Recognition must be given to the development of the various elements and changes affecting the general background in which the contract is made. These include technologic, economic, and social modifications that today's enlightened managers and nonmanagers recognize and accept.

LABOR MANAGEMENT RELATIONS ACT OF 1947

A long list of labor laws make up the legal background upon which current management-union cooperation is administered. But for our purpose, the provisions of the Labor Management Relations Act of 1947, commonly referred to as the Taft-Hartley Act, and the Landrum-Griffin Act of 1959 can be considered as making up the current labor legislation. There are also important state labor laws. We are omitting them, however, in order to keep this discussion a reasonable length. The Landrum-Griffin Act of 1959, among other things, permitted employees to file with the government complaints about the acts of their union leaders. Most of the complaints to date have dealt with questions pertaining to voting by union members in union affairs, and the misuse of the dues by union officers.

The Labor Management Relations Act of 1947 is the important legislation that sets forth the major provisions of management-labor cooperation. By this law, a National Labor Relations Board (NLRB) was established with the power to hear testimony, render decisions, and decide the appropriate unit for purposes of collective bargaining. The board serves mainly in a judiciary capacity. A general counsel and his staff prosecute the cases brought before the board. Among the other important provisions of this law are (1) unfair labor practices, (2) strike controls, and (3) checks on unions. These provisions will now be discussed.

The Taft-Hartley Act forbids unfair labor practices either by the employer or by unions or their agents. Unfair labor practices by an employer include (1) interfering with or restraining employees from forming or joining a labor union, (2) dominating or influencing a labor organization, (3) discriminating in the hiring or in the conditions of employment of any employee because he is a member of a union, (4) terminating employment or discriminating against any employee for any charge made or testimony given under this law, and (5) refusing to bargain collectively with representatives of his employees.

Practices which constitute unfair labor practices by unions or their agents include (1) coercing or restraining employees in connection with their joining a union, (2) charging "excessive or discriminatory" union initiation fees (the meaning of "excessive or discriminatory" is determined by the labor board in cases where there is an authorized union shop contract), (3) refusing to bargain collectively with the employer, (4) participating in jurisdictional strikes, and (5) practicing "featherbedding," i.e., making the employer pay for services not performed.

Charges of unfair labor practices on the part of either employer or union are investigated, complaints issued, and prosecution carried on before the National Labor Relations Board by the general counsel, who has exclusive authority to prosecute unfair labor practices. He is appointed by the President of the United States and has general supervision over all attorneys employed by the board, except trial examiners and legal assistants to board members.

Basing its decision on the preponderance of evidence and testimony, the board decides whether any defendant named in the complaint is guilty of an unfair labor practice. If he is not guilty, the findings are stated, and an order is issued dismissing the complaint. If he is guilty, the board states its findings and causes a cease and desist order, prohibiting the continuation of the unfair practice, to be served on the guilty party. For enforcement of its orders, the board has the power to petition the Circuit Court of Appeals with jurisdiction where the unfair labor practice occurred.

Under the subject of strike controls, the Taft-Hartley Act provides that 60 days' notice must be given the other party before the normal termination of a labor contract. The Federal Mediation and Conciliation Service must be notified at least 30 days after the 60-day notice if no agreement is reached. This provision is, of course, intended to help settle the differences of opinion. Lockouts and strikes are prohibited during the notice period. There is no compulsory arbitration or court injunction right against a legitimate noncritical strike, i.e., one not threatening "national health and safety" or affecting an entire industry.

In contrast, threatening lockouts or strikes affecting "national health and safety" or an entire industry may be delayed 80 days by the President in this manner: A board of inquiry may be appointed to determine the facts involved in the dispute. A report stating these facts, along with each party's statement of its position, is filed with the Federal Mediation and Conciliation Service, and the contents are made known to the public. In addition, the President at this time may, through the Attorney General, seek a court injunction against the lockout or strike. If the injunction is issued, there follows a period of 60 days in which to bring about a settlement. If this is not reached, the National Labor Relations Board holds, within the ensuing 15 days, a company-by-company election on each employer's last offer of settlement and certifies same within five days to the Attorney General, who then moves to dissolve the injunction. Then, the President submits a comprehensive report of the proceedings to Congress, along with any recommendation which he deems fitting and proper for appropriate action.

With reference to checks on unions, the law provides that a union may seek an election under NLRB supervision or file an unfair labor practice charge with the board. For such action, the union must previously file (1) pertinent union information and (2) noncommunist affidavits by each officer of the union.

The pertinent union information is filed annually with the Secretary of Labor. The report must include name, title, compensation, and allowances for each of the union's three principal officers and for any other officer or agent of the union if the aggregate compensation and allowances of any one of these persons exceeded $5,000 for the preceding year. The report must also include the manner of election or appointment of these officers or agents; the amount of initiation fees and regular dues; a statement showing the procedure followed for such things as qualifications for union membership, levying of assessments, authorization for bargaining demands, for strikes, for disbursement of union funds, and for the basis for expulsion of members; and a report showing receipts and expenditures for the fiscal year and total assets and liabilities at the end of the fiscal year. All union members have a right to a copy of their union's financial report.

The affidavits by union officers can be filed either contemporaneously with a union action privileged by the act or within the preceding 12-month period. The affidavit is a sworn written statement signifying that the union officer is not a member or affiliate of the Communist Party and does not believe in, belong to, or support any organization believing in or teaching the overthrow of the United States government by force or by illegal or unconstitutional methods.

There are additional important provisions of the act that merit mentioning. They include:

1. Union shop agreements must be in accordance with the prevailing state law and are void in states that forbid them.

2. An employee or a group of employees can petition that the union's authorization to enter into a union shop contract be withdrawn; such a petition must contain the signatures of 30 percent of the employees

represented by the union. However, only one election on union security can be held each year.

3. In instances of authorized union shop contracts, the failure of a member to pay union dues and initiation fee is the only cause for loss of good standing with the union for which an employer can be forced to discharge an employee.

4. Union dues checkoff is allowed only with the employee's written consent.

5. If the majority of professional employees desire a union, they can be represented, if they wish, by a union other than that representing the production workers.

6. The individual employee can present grievances directly to his supervisor, provided the union representative is informed and given an opportunity to be present. Settlement of the grievance can be made if such settlement is not contrary to any terms of the existing union contract.

7. The employer can refuse to bargain with a union of foremen or supervisors. They can have their union, but the employer need not bargain with them if he does not choose to do so.

8. Unions as well as employers can sue and be sued for violations of contract under this act. Judgments against unions must be collected from them, not from the individual employees.

HANDLING CONTROVERSIES

Ideally, the manager and the union representative should solve their differences by means of interpreting the labor contract, bargaining, or mutual agreement. In practice, however, this does not always take place. Hence, to handle controversies, several methods are available, including the following:

By mediation. Both parties agree to use a third party, or mediator, in order to compromise or reach an agreement. He may relay one party's opinion to the other or act as a chairman in getting the parties together to relate their beliefs and opinions. In addition, the mediator may define the basis of the dispute and show the legal meaning of the agreement, thus indirectly demonstrating how settlement might be reached.

By conciliation. Each party may ask for a conciliator who serves as an intermediate and seeks to settle the dispute. In contrast to that of the mediator, the work of the conciliator is aggressive; he may be said to take the offensive. The conciliator may induce one party to accept certain requests of the other or may give advice as to the manner of settling the dispute. To bring about agreement, conciliators depend upon such things as their ability, prestige, and knowledge of all facts in the case. They have no legal power to compel acceptance of any terms.

By arbitration. The parties may use voluntary arbitration to settle their differences. To do this, both parties agree to submit the case to a neutral, impartial third party or umpire. It is usually agreed that the arbitrator's findings will be accepted as final.[2]

In actual practice, the terms "mediation" and "conciliation" are used synonymously. As previously stated, the Taft-Hartley Act provides that a 30-day notice of a change in or termination of a labor contract must be filed with the Federal Mediation and Conciliation Service. This makes it possible for the service to get the differences settled before an open break has occurred.

IMPROVING MANAGEMENT-LABOR RELATIONS

The current status of management-labor relations can be considered quite satisfactory, but improvements are possible. To meet better the challenge of bargaining, advance greater harmony, and gain greater management-union cooperation, the following recommendations are made:

1. *Utilize competent managers more intensively.* Application of the best minds is necessary to find the superior means of bettering management-union relations. Time has brought improvement, but much remains to be done. Managers need to take the offensive and acquire an enlightened view on their role in collective bargaining. They should find out the real reasons behind the union demands. Progress in the following areas would be highly beneficial: bettering the communication with and motivation of employees, smoothing out the business cycle, improving management techniques, training more efficient employees, and broadening the educational background of managers and of labor leaders.

2. *Establish mutual agreement on rights of management.* Managers desire freedom to meet their responsibilities and resent any restrictions upon functions which they believe essential for performing their job. Traditionally, managers want no restrictions on their right to hire, fire, discipline, and maintain order and efficiency. On the other hand, unions feel that one of their main functions concerns the welfare of their members. They are interested in all matters which involve the employee; conditions of employment, they reason, are of vital concern to them. Experience shows that the initiative and firm policies taken by

---

[2] K. Braun, *The Settlement of Industrial Disputes* (Philadelphia: Blakiston Co., 1944), p. 29.

"Arbitration," as discussed here, applies to reaching a contract agreement and is not the common type of arbitration which deals with the interpretation and application of existing contracts to specific disputes.

managers determine to a significant degree what action the union takes. It is possible to include in the contract the principal managerial rights and specify these as managerial functions; but acceptance by the union is a debatable question and depends upon individual circumstances and precedents, and the character of the rights. There are some who feel that a policy of specifying managerial functions has a limiting effect, since unions might claim participation in matters not specifically stated. However, this might be handled by stating that all existing functions now carried out by managers shall remain functions of management.

3. *Recognize and reconcile the aims of managers and of unions.* Too frequently the goals of managers are unknown to unions and likewise, the goals of unions are a mystery to managers. The goals of each should be identified and analyzed. When this is done, they appear compatible and able to exist in harmony. Such a disclosure forms a solid foundation for building better relations and understanding. The goals of managers usually include (1) an equitable income for the owners, (2) a reasonable income for contingencies, expansion, and improvements, (3) a good reputation for products and services, (4) a reputation as a good place to work, and (5) a favorable attitude by the public. Among the union's chief aims are (1) security of employment, (2) wages consistent with a decent standard of living and commensurate with the quality and quantity of work output, (3) consultation and opportunity for suggestions in shaping policies, (4) employee recognition and status for work well done, and (5) good working conditions.

4. *Practice empathy by managers and by union representatives.* Each should strive to recognize fully the problems of the other. Neither party should ask for concessions which, if granted, would jeopardize the existence of the other. Both should seek for something workable, since any other approach leads to strife. It is simply recognizing the facts of office life—that managers are here to stay and also that unions are here to stay.

5. *Accept complete responsibilities by managers and by union representatives.* This is fundamental. Both managers and unions should be capable, willing to accept and to assume their respective and complete responsibilities. Agreements made in good faith should be carried out, and any subsequent adjustments found desirable should be made in accordance with the mutually agreed upon procedure.

6. *Recognize all interested parties.* It is well to note that there are actually *three, not two,* interested parties in a labor contract: (1) the employees, represented by the union; (2) the owners, represented by managerial personnel; and (3) the consumers, or general public. The negotiators are usually only the managers and the union representatives,

but the agreements they reach should be consistent with the public interest. Disagreements resulting in strikes or shutdowns obviously affect public interest. Likewise, agreements which are contrary to the public interest can be very damaging; although more subtle, they can probably have a greater effect upon certain members of society than upon the initial disputants.

7. *Develop closer association among managers, union representatives, and employees.* Managers should know the union representatives, union representatives should know the managers, and both should know the employees. They should know each other as fellow human beings working together. A spirit of cooperation and understanding should prevail; for all three are bound together, and they must strive for mutual, not separate, survival.

8. *Establish a mutually agreeable basis for conducting collective bargaining.* Most managers would like to operate on the familiar business basis. To them, the process is orderly, and contracts represent agreements satisfactory to both, which in case of violation means redresses enforceable by court action. However, evidence seems to indicate that in some instances, unions are not certain that the traditional business code is the best medium. They are driven by a passion for improvement of the employees' lot and, in many respects, believe collective bargaining and the attainment of satisfactory management-union cooperation are more in the nature of a social and political procedure than a business procedure. For collective bargaining improvement to take place it appears mandatory that these extremes be brought together in some way or a mutually agreed basis be established.

In conclusion, it can be stated that progress in the above eight areas will require time. They are essentially long-range developments and both managers and labor representatives must allow time for ideas to be absorbed. Improvements do not just happen overnight; they evolve; they take time.

CHAPTER NINE

OFFICE PERSONNEL

DYNAMICS

The greatest mistake you can make in life is
to be continually fearing you will make one.
—Elbert G. Hubbard

OFFICE organization and office motivation, both engrossed with office personnel, are vibrant, living entities because people and their work relationships are highly dynamic. Change takes place whether planned or desired. Change occurs because people are what they are, because organizing is what it is, and because motivating is what it is. Work demands change; relationships and interactions of employees change; and the views of both managers and nonmanagers change. This dynamic state of affairs is recognized by the astute management member who strives to utilize the inevitable changes to update his organization, to maximize his personnel utilization, and to satisfy current demands of his group members.

For clarity, let us first look at these dynamics from the viewpoint of organization, or the group idea as identified in Chapter 1, and follow this by a discussion from the viewpoint of personnel, or what has been considered the approach of the individual. But to reiterate, it must always be remembered that organizing and personnel are closely interrelated. Office personnel dynamics are brought about jointly by changes in organizing and changes in employees.

RESPONSIBILITY FOR ORGANIZATION CHANGES

Too often, an existent organization expands or contracts without any genuine direction or guidance by the managers. New functions and new personnel are added and the organization just grows, or in contrast, functions are combined, peculiar organization relationships established, and personnel placed on jobs requiring but a small portion of their capacities. Or a needed organizational adjustment may be postponed indefinitely—the outmoded organization being permitted to give rise to difficult managerial problems. More precisely, this failure to recognize organization dynamics and utilize them constructively leads to these undesirable conditions:

1. The functions become disproportionate in their relationship to each other when judged by the relative importance of each function to the objectives of the enterprise.

2. Important functions are neglected, or they are subordinated to other functions; either condition makes it difficult to carry out the requisite activities.

3. New functions of a planning nature which might greatly strengthen the organization are ignored.

4. Capable men are confined to mediocre jobs.

5. Authority relationships become blurred; differences arise over who is supposed to decide what.

6. The necessary coordination among the major functions is decreased, since the personnel for each major function tend to stress their individual activity exclusively.

All things considered, the organization used is the result of managers' thinking and implementing in this area of management. Especially is this true of top managers, for their attitudes and thoughts tend to mold the organization structure adopted. They cast the die and decide, sometimes arbitrarily, what the organization pattern will be and when and where changes in it will be made. To some degree, top managers are influenced by their subordinates regarding what changes in the existent structure should be made. But in most cases, organizational suggestions initiated by subordinates are conditioned by them in order to insure approval by the top managers. The location, timing, and extent of any organizational modification is regulated ultimately by the top managers.

Fortunately, the growing practice among enterprises of updating and improving the organization structure at regular intervals is being recognized as advantageous. For example, in some companies, this task is assigned to one individual within the organization. He works closely with the various management members, discussing possible organizational improvements with the managers who would be affected by such changes, and encouraging them to offer their ideas and participate in developing needed organizational improvements. Having an individual to head up the activity of possible organizational changes is an effective way to insure that attention will be given this important work. A number of large, well-known companies have established a special organization unit for the sole purpose of studying and recommending organization changes and improvements. They report excellent results for these "organization evaluation" units.

ORGANIZATION CONTINUITY

The continuity of an organization is conditioned chiefly by (1) the work—both its flow and its type—and (2) the time element. A relatively stable and continuing organization usually results when the flow of work is steady. Modifications in organization structure are likely to be minor and infrequent. The line as well as the staff functions are usually well defined and known. On the other hand, when demand for the products or services is irregular, the predominant idea is usually to meet current requirements; and generally, the organization is of a line type, with relatively few staff functions. It tends to be a "nothing or all" existence.

Under the consideration of type of work, assume that office A handles the same work day in and day out and that office B handles a certain type of work X for a part of a month, work Y for another part of a month, and work Z for still another part of a month. The structural organization of office A will probably differ from that of office B, and the personnel must be attuned to changes periodically as a normal state of affairs. Office A probably will emphasize staff elements. Office B, on the other hand, will tend toward a line type of organization in which most employees can perform several activities with equal skill.

Organizational continuity is also affected by the time element. A structure set up temporarily to accomplish an emergency task might be far different from one set up to exist over a long period of time. Organization structures having little continuity are usually very simple. An office group to handle registrations for a one-day convention might well be organized quite differently than a group organized to handle tax registrations. Or consider the example of a crowd of people organized to put out a fire in the neighborhood. They probably will be organized far differently from the firemen of the local fire department. The crowd of people will probably organize so that every member does something physical to put out the fire. It is unlikely that there would be any staff advisory members. Speed of action would be paramount and at the conclusion of the fire, the group would be dissolved. In contrast, the local fire department probably utilizes not only direct fire fighters but also a trained staff of experts in carrying out the task of fire fighting. Through time, the fire department has developed an efficient, highly coordinated organizational structure. And it is permanent—it is not dismantled after each fire-fighting experience.

NEED FOR ORGANIZATIONAL BALANCE

Organizing, to be effective, must represent a balance among the various activities in relation to their real worth and contribution. An office is not all billing, all tabulating, all procedures analyzing, all filing, or all anything else. It is a proper balance and blending among the many activities believed essential. The effective organizer thinks in these terms, yet he recognizes that organization dynamics has a significant effect upon the maintenance of this balance.

Normal changes within an organization take place in different areas and to different degrees. This results from current popular interest, research and development, and personal managerial intent. To illustrate, the records retention unit spurts in size due to a strong swing in managerial thinking on its importance; or systems and procedures develops into a central activity of those concerned with paper work processing, and organizational units within which this type of work is performed are expanded and given greater authority.

The result of these localized changes may tend to make the entire organization unbalanced. In some instances, the strengthened unit needed just that to place it in proper balance with the other organizational units. But frequently, the strengthening does not stop at the point of balance; it continues until a state of imbalance among the units is again present.

The meaning of organizational balance is subject to a great many interpretations. Good organizing maintains the relative importance of the various functions. Too frequently, however, managers continue to improve what is already relatively effective. Bettering the weak areas would be more helpful from the viewpoint of the entire organization. An important part of the problem is not to place all strong managers of the enterprise in one or a few organizational units. Success begets success. Commonly, the strong manager tends to attract trainees with the greatest managerial potential, and the more proficient manager tends to develop good managers under him.

In analyzing an office organization, it may be found that certain activities such as corresponding and billing appear grossly overemphasized relative to their importance in view of all the other office activities. Further study may reveal that the past experience and work of the office manager was in the area now seemingly too large or being given too much emphasis. Why is this? Because there is a human tendency by managers to emphasize and manage well those activities in which they are most interested and experienced. If the office manager "knows" corresponding, this work will tend to be organized and managed well. On the other hand, if he knows very little about office personnel research, this activity may be somewhat neglected and not developed to its required relative importance.

MAJOR INFLUENCES BRINGING ORGANIZATION CHANGE

From what has already been stated, it is evident that there are many factors which bring about change in an organization. To exhaust a list of causes is beyond our purpose here. Excluding the change in personnel itself, there are three major influences which represent important considerations in organization dynamics. These three influences are (1) the process and machines used, (2) the relationships followed, and (3) the degree of centralization practiced.

PROCESS AND MACHINES USED

The process utilized quite often determines the main components of the organization structure. In the handling of a purchase order, for example, receiving, costing, billing, and mailing may contribute the main components. However, research and concentrated efforts for improvement may evolve a different process for the handling of purchase orders. Information in a different form or time sequence may be adopted to reduce costs. It is also possible that some computer means or duplicating improvement might revolutionize the old process into one that is different and brand new. This, in turn, would mean organizational changes.

Closely allied with process changes are the machines used. Mechanization may use the identical process, but it may perform the work in such a manner and at such speed that changes in the organizational pattern are necessary. Certainly, when the office work is being accomplished largely by manual means and is changed to one of mechanical processing, organizational modifications are in order. Mechanization may eliminate certain functions and change others, resulting in the need for different people, at least in the sense of the displaced people being retrained for the new work, and new organizational relationships being established.

THE RELATIONSHIPS FOLLOWED

There is an old saying that "authority clusters around the person willing to accept it." The employee of managerial competence, ambition, and desire for authority tends to acquire additional wanted authority. Hence, over a period, authority tends to be increased by such individuals; and as a result, organization relationships change, at first in practice, and ultimately formally, in keeping with conditions as they have developed.

In Chapter 3, it was pointed out that for a small organization many functions are usually grouped into each organization unit, the total number of such units is small, a line type organization is used, and the number of relationships is relatively low. In contrast, when few functions are in each organization unit, the number of units is large, a line and staff type of organization is used, and the relationships are relatively high in number. In either of these cases when the relationships are altered, there is a necessity of change in the organization structure. There can, in fact, be an organization change caused by a modification in relationships only; a change in functions or in their grouping or in personnel is not necessary.

THE DEGREE OF CENTRALIZATION PRACTICED

A key contributor to organization change is the movement either to or from centralization. As already stated the current trend is toward more and more centralization of office work. In and of itself this makes for organization changes. But the degree of centralization should not be determined by following blindly what others may be doing. The soundest approach is to make an objective study within the given enterprise. For this purpose, a four-step program can be followed:

1. *Determine the major centers of office work activity.* Essentially this is an inventory showing, by centers, the name, location, number of employees, major work performed, quantities of work, and equipment utilized. From these data, it is possible to identify the areas offering the greatest potential for improvement. The use of a simple form such as that shown in Figure 32 is helpful in this recording work.

2. *Ascertain the productive efficiency of these centers.* Find out if any relationship exists between the volume of work processed by a group and the work output per person in that group. In general, a high volume of available work per person is related to high individual productivity. This results partly from the fact that there must be a sufficient work volume to keep an employee busy throughout the work period. Figure 33 shows that for a given enterprise, the greater the number of billings processed, the higher the employee productivity or billings processed per employee. Each dot in the figure represents a district office of the company. In the case of two district offices, the number of billings processed is about 420,

CLERICAL FUNCTIONS INVENTORY					
COMPANY:		INFORMATION BY:		DATE:	
WORK GROUP	LOCATION AND DEPARTMENT	NUMBER OF EMPLOYEES		MAJOR WORK PERFORMED	OFFICE MACHINES AND EQUIPMENT USED
		SUPERVISORY	NON-SUPERV'Y		

FIG. 32.   Recording form to simplify inventory of clerical functions.

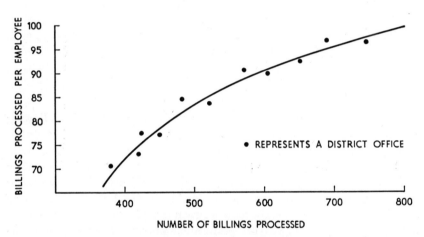

FIG. 33.   Relationship between average productivity per employee performing billing processing and number of billings processed for each of 11 district offices.

and the corresponding productivity per employee is 73 and 77, respectively. When the volume of work is higher, at 700 or 750, as in other district offices, the productivity jumps to 97. This suggests gains to be derived by centralizing all billing work; but before this conclusion can be reached, the analyst should conduct similar investigations for other clerical work performed in the district offices, such as credit and collections, and accounts receivable, to determine if a similar pattern emerges. From this range of information, the feasibility of consolidation can be demonstrated.

3. *Establish an optimum number of major office work centers.* We are trying to answer the questions: To what degree should the centralization be pursued? Do you collapse office work done in 11 district sales offices to six or three regional office service centers, or some number in between? In some cases, the optimum size can be determined for the data utilized in step No. 2 by noting the volume point at which definite plateauing takes place, that is, employee productivity remains constant regardless of the work volume. Using this optimum work volume as a base, the number of district offices can be determined. But this mathematical answer usually must be qualified by nonmeasurable factors, such as the potential office mechanization, the need of communication between the organizational units, the cost of conversion, employee training required, and the vulnerability and risk involved should the centralized units become incapacitated due to equipment breakdown, strikes, or disaster.

4. *Decide on the location of the major office work centers.* Top managers normally make this decision, keeping in mind certain criteria among which are the present organization structure, the personnel involved, the availability and cost of labor, and the likely direction of the company's future growth and paper work requirements.

FORMAT FOR REORGANIZING

Work of reorganizing should follow a definite pattern. The following format is effective:

1. *Make an inventory of the present organization.* It is absolutely essential to know the precise identity of the organization structure being reorganized. Assumptions and guesses in this respect lead to unnecessary trouble and work. The correct name of each organizational unit, the exact work performed, the employees performing what work in each unit, the line and the staff authority relationships existing among all the units should be carefully ascertained and set down in writing.

2. *Write a description for each job.* Although it requires much time and detailed effort, preparing a written description of each job is usually extremely helpful. In no other way will the reorganizer fully realize the exact content of the various work segments and how they are related. Preparing written descriptions also greatly assists in securing clues as to what work might better be placed other than where it is in the present organization.

3. *Analyze current organization, and evaluate proposed changes.* This step is guided mainly by the objectives of the entire organization and the part that each component is expected to contribute to the goal accom-

plishment. Knowledge of the people available to perform the various tasks is also essential. This can be gained by researching the personnel records and talking with the supervisors or with the employees themselves. Some means of recording information in a logical order should be followed. Data common to all employees should be obtained so that reasonable comparisons can be made.

From all this information, the proposed organization is gradually evolved. Several different ideas, encompassing different work divisions, people, and relationships, are tentatively drawn up. Subsequently, each arrangement is evaluated, noting what appear to be its strong and its weak points, the probable hurdles involved in putting it into force, the effect upon the personnel to be changed, the possibility of acquiring needed new personnel, the training which will be required, and similar considerations. Tentative arrangements should be discussed with various management members and affected personnel to gain their appraisals and exchange reactions regarding the advantages and disadvantages to be incurred and the consensus regarding what should be done. Based on the results of this overall investigation, the decision is made as to the makeup of the reorganization to be used.

4. *Determine the phases or steps to be taken from the present to the proposed organization.* It may be deemed wise to institute the reorganization at once. In situations where an extremely inefficient or costly organizational structure exists, it may be best to implement the change without delay. However, in many cases, the gradual shifting from the present to the ultimate organization takes place in several phases or steps. Normally, this makes for greater acceptance by the employees, who will go along with a small change but will balk if the modification is too large or believed radical from their viewpoint. Individual situations may govern the timing of the change. For example, the retirement or resignation of a key executive may signal the most opportune time to adopt change. However, regardless of the reason, in each instance the plan of what is to be done and by whom should be worked out in advance. To reorganize without adequate predetermination and study usually leads to poor results.

Figure 34 illustrates the phases of reorganization that might be followed by a company whose present office organization is like that shown by the top diagram. Note that seven managerial chiefs report to the office manager. It is desired to reduce the number of chiefs reporting directly to the office manager, to install and use a computer, and to consolidate relative functions in order to get a more tightly knit and effective organization structure.

The first phase in this reorganization is shown by the middle

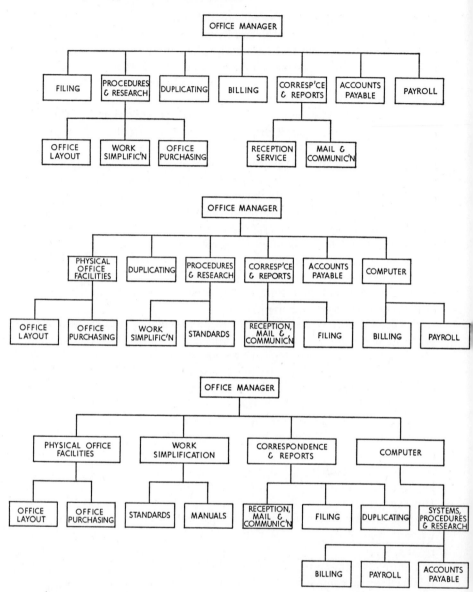

FIG. 34.   Phase charts are commonly used in reorganizing. The present organization is illustrated by the top chart. The first phase of changes to be made is shown
by the middle chart. Subsequently, the organization of the middle chart is changed
to that shown by the bottom phase chart.

illustration of Figure 34. Procedures and research has been given the subfunctions of work simplification and the newly created standards section. Under the new unit of physical office facilities is placed office layout and office purchasing. The correspondence and reports unit now includes filing along with reception, mail, and communicative services consolidated into one subunit. The computer unit is added and initially will process data in connection will billing and payroll. Accounts payable remains a separate unit, as does duplicating; the head of each reports directly to the office manager.

The second and final phase consists of adding systems to the procedures and research unit and transferring this enlarged unit to the computer section. Work simplification with standards and a manuals unit under it report directly to the office manager. Duplicating is transferred and becomes a subunit under correspondence and reports, while accounts payable is placed under the computer organizational unit.

5. *Take necessary reorganization action.* The last step is to put the reorganization into action. Once it is decided what changes to make and a time schedule established, definite action should be taken. To hesitate or display indecisiveness can hamper the entire reorganization. A positive viewpoint, fairness, and pointing out the "reasons why" generally assist in getting good results.

It is important to give the reorganization time to prove itself. Time is required for people to adjust to new assignments, become familiar with new authority relationships, and utilize new formal channels of communication. All managers should be thoroughly indoctrinated in the reorganization, be able to answer questions concerning it, publicize its advantages, and counsel any employee in need of such help. Successful reorganization plans always include these important follow-up features.

Specific attention should be called to the fact that the above list does not include copying the organization of another enterprise in a similar business. Organizing is highly personalized and should be tailor-made for the specific objectives, type of work, and people of a given enterprise. Needs and circumstances vary. Basic guides are available for the construction of an effective organization and should be used in keeping with the basic requirements. The work is similar to the architect designing a building. The best architect does not copy an existing building. He employs basic guides of building and engineering and creates a structure that meets the specific and personal needs of his client.

CHANGES IN PERSONNEL

Probably the most significant and common cause of office personnel dynamics is change in the personnel or in the people who are employed by the enterprise. This change in personnel comes about in three different ways: (1) the manager believes a shifting of certain present personnel to different jobs or to different organization units will prove advantageous; (2) the manager recognizes that some personnel have changed and desires to utilize better their possible contributions; or (3) the manager is confronted with the problem of labor turnover—some employees leave, and replacements must be found for them, or the employee requirements of the office change.

Certain types of people tend to work together effectively as a group, while others never seem to reach the level of expected cooperation. The reasons are many; but presumably most important are differences in personalities, capacities, and relationships among the group's members. Various predetermined personnel measurements and devices can be employed to place employees better, but trial-and-error, probationary, or temporary placement approaches are widely used. Nothing, it seems, completely takes the place of actually trying the employee out and observing what is achieved from this trial. This shuffling of personnel makes for organizational changes and is done in the interests not only of employee social satisfaction but also for production efficiency.

Most managers recognize the fundamental truth that with time, their employees change. They acquire new knowledge, new skills, new interests, and new attitudes. This is inevitable; in fact, it is promoted by managers in management development programs and many efforts of motivation. But it is perhaps more important that people change because it is a natural evolutionary process which takes place as a person increases in age, participates in more experiences, and reflects on life and its meaning. An office job satisfactory to a young woman of 20 probably will not satisfy her when she reaches 26. She will seek a change, and the alert manager will recognize this and do something about it. Later, at age 35, it could well be that no job in industry will satisfy her, as her interests and desires are now centered on work in connection with her own family. The point here is that no person remains static. Some change more rapidly than others, but change they do. Managers, in their organizing work, should take these personnel changes into account; and this means the organization structure will be dynamic.

Sooner or later, all offices have the problem of employee replacement due to the normal state of affairs of some employees leaving the office or the employee requirements of the office changing as the office work either expands or contracts. A basic need of every office is to supply and to maintain a satisfactory working force. To do this, likely candidates must be located and those best qualified selected and hired. This brings up the important subject areas of recruiting and selecting office employees, and the next several pages will be devoted to a discussion of them.

RECRUITING

The recruitment of employees is a permanent activity. Increased emphasis is placed upon this work during peak business periods, but the problem of securing the right employees confronts most offices most of the time. There are always separations because of marriage, illness, voluntary leaves, terminations, and death.

Recruiting has four major aspects: (1) the determining of future needs, (2) the evaluating of the recruiting process for different types of office jobs, (3) the establishing of contacts helpful for referrals of candidates, and (4) the preparing and distributing of appropriate material used to promote recruiting efforts. Knowing the quantity and quality of candidates to seek and when to seek them constitutes the first requirement of effective recruiting. People of the skill, attitude, and interest that the office requires should set the background for recruiting efforts. Following this, attention should be directed to the sources utilized and the contacts established. Many office managers have found that appropriate recruiting literature is definitely helpful in aiding recruiting efforts.

Limited data reveal that the number of applicants hired to the number rejected is in the ratio of 1 to 7, and that over $200 is spent for each office employee hired. These data suggest that recruiting can be improved. What can be done? Probably foremost is the use of more accurate and complete job specifications. When the job requirements are vague, the likelihood of finding a satisfactory candidate is considerably lessened. No available source can supply its maximum recruiting assistance when the information supplied is insufficient and not clearly stated. Another improvement possibility is the avoidance of delay in hiring the likely candidate. In too many cases, a qualified candidate is lost because of a lack of promptness in dealing with the applicant from the time of application to the time the decision to hire or not to hire is rendered. A third area is developing the reputation of the particular office as being a good place to work. The office possessing this valuable public good will commonly has a satisfactory group from which outstanding candidates can be selected.

SOURCES OF OFFICE HELP

Generally speaking, a variety of labor sources is desirable and needed to meet recruitment goals. The "best" source usually must be qualified regarding the type of office job, the geographical location, the prominence of the company, and the skill with which the recruiter uses a particular source. The proper personnel viewpoint is to work with a number of different sources of office help. Better people usually can be selected if there is a group from which to choose.

Among the more common sources are:

1. *Persons recommended by present employees.* This is usually a very good source, but caution must be exercised to avoid favoritism. Some companies post notices on bulletin boards encouraging employees to recommend friends who might be seeking employment.

2. *Former employees.* This group constitutes an excellent source. However, careful screening and selection techniques are required to avoid a "come and go" atmosphere. Frequently, satisfactory part-time employees can be obtained from this source.

3. *New employees.* The person just hired usually knows somebody else who is looking for a job. Satisfactory results are usually obtained if candidates are put through the regular selection channels.

4. *Employment agencies.* It is well to utilize this source. Some agencies are public, others are private. The former charge no fee; the latter do, and the charge commonly is made to the employer. Agencies have broad contacts and experience; they try to supply likely candidates for vacancies.

5. *Schools—including vocational advisory boards.* This is one of the better and larger sources of office employees. Some companies keep in close touch with high schools, business colleges, and universities, and send representatives to talk with students about to graduate. Many schools have placement offices and will cooperate fully with prospective employers. It is well to develop schools as a source of office help. The candidates usually have formal training but limited business experience.

6. *Institutions for the rehabilitation of handicapped persons.* Frequently, very capable people can be secured from this source.

7. *Voluntary applicants.* It is a good practice always to see people who come in looking for a job. Frequently, this source offers excellent personnel, but it cannot be relied upon as the sole source of help.

8. *Advertising.* Newspaper, radio, and television advertising are effective media for securing a number of candidates. Good coverage is usually obtained; but all respondents will not be fully qualified, and the normal weeding-out process must be used.

SELECTION OF OFFICE HELP

Choice of a candidate is normally based on a comparison between (1) what the job requires for successful execution and (2) what the applicant has to offer. For the most part, the better the balance between these two factors, the better the selection work, and the more likely is the attainment of a satisfactory working force. Under job requirements are such attributes as the amount of formal education, knowledge, experience, and physical considerations. Under what the applicant offers are his fund of knowledge, experience, intelligence, physical attributes, and personality. This matching effort, however, must not be thought of as an exacting operation. On the contrary, it is quite flexible. Job requirements should be used as a guide. Frequently, a satisfactory person does not have the *exact* qualifications desired; but with time and experience, he may well prove satisfactory on the job.

The use of vocational requirements facilitates the selection. For example, the suggested minimum vocational requirements for the job of beginning stenographer might be established at ability to type at a rate of 55 words per minute on straight copy material for a ten-minute period, with five errors or less; to perform shorthand writing at 100 words per minute; to transcribe notes of unfamiliar material at the rate of 35 words per minute for a ten-minute period, and to produce work of mailable quality; to transcribe from a machine, at the rate of 10–12 letters per hour each letter consisting of two to three paragraphs. Progress is being made by various associations in getting office managers to request employees who meet definite vocational standards and in getting schools to train students toward these standards.

TOOLS OF PERSONNEL SELECTION

There are a number of selection tools that assist in deciding which candidate should be placed in what job of an office organization structure. Discussion here includes the tools of (1) application form, (2) interview, (3) references, (4) physical examination, and (5) tests.

1. *Application form. The application form is a written record providing a means of securing and maintaining the more obvious personnel information, such as identification, education, work history, and activities of the applicant.* It is particularly helpful for selection purposes. Sufficient information should be obtained, but superfluous information should be avoided. All questions asked should serve a definite purpose in evaluating the candidate's possible value to the office.

For the higher-level jobs, it is often quite helpful to ask several questions designed to gain some insight into the candidate's general attitude toward life and his ability to write and to organize material. To illustrate, questions such as the following might be asked: "In narrative form, give us a résumé of your major accomplishments, hopes, and ambition." "Will you tell us about your special qualifications not covered elsewhere in this application?" "What unusual business situations have you encountered, and what did you do about them?"

2. *Interviews.* One of the basic tools in the selection process is the interview. It provides the opportunity for meeting the applicant and observing his verbal ability, appearance, general personality, and attitude, as well as the chance to "get together and talk it over." The face-to-face meeting with the applicant offers possibilities of information afforded by no other means.

The objectives of the employment interview are to exchange information and to make a favorable impression upon the applicant. Unless these conditions are accomplished, the interview is not wholly satisfactory. The exchange of information is essential to intelligent selection. Creating a favorable impression reflects the interviewer's ability to gain public goodwill by securing a favorable attitude of the applicant toward the office, whether he is hired or not.

To assist interviewing, it is a good practice for the interviewer to have a list of items he wishes to cover. The accuracy and quality standards on previous jobs held by the candidate, the supervisory practices liked, and the grades received in school are illustrative of areas to cover that will make for effective interviewing. Second, rating charts can be used. By this means, a written record of the relative intensities of the important factors is made by the interviewer. A third interviewing aid is oral trade questions. An idea of the candidate's competency is obtained through the use of these questions, which are concerned with names of office machines, office operations, general knowledge of office jobs, and the like. Fourth, an interviewer's guide, designed to help secure essential information, can be used. The interviewer asks the questions on the guide and records the answers given by the applicant as favorable or unfavorable. Fifth, interviewing practices shown by experience to be effective should be followed. These include:

a) Putting the applicant and yourself at ease.

b) Explaining clearly what the job is—the duties, responsibilities, chances for promotion, working conditions, and so forth. If possible, read or let the candidate read the job description.

c) Using language appropriate to the educational and experience background of the applicant—language that does not reveal your own attitude.

d) Encouraging the applicant to talk by asking questions that begin with *why, when,* and *how.* Avoid questions that can be answered by a "Yes" or "No."

e) Interrupting the applicant only when what is being said is irrelevant. Start speaking after the applicant has paused for at least ten seconds.

f) Letting the applicant ask questions.

g) Granting sufficient time for the interview, but not prolonging it to the point of boredom or useless repetition.

h) Keeping your interviews fresh. Periodically change the questions and the sequence in which they are asked.

3. *References*.   Managers usually like to obtain information on the applicant from previous employers and responsible persons currently acquainted with him. Reference checking is a helpful means in appraising not only the candidate's cooperation and dependability but also the candidate's probable skill, interests, and abilities. On the other hand, there are many who believe references are frequently unreliable. Members of this school claim inaccurate evaluations are provided; either excessive praise or excessive criticism is supplied.

The value of references depends upon the knowledge and character of the person supplying the reference information. Qualifications include being fully familiar with the demands of the job, knowing the candidate extremely well, supplying information with absolute honesty, and exercising sound evaluating judgment. These qualifications appear to be filled best by professional people and by former employers.

In a great majority of cases, agreement on these points exists:

a) References from former employers are more reliable than those supplied by personal friends of the candidate. Former employers can verify dates of employment, salaries, type and quality of work performed, and attendance record.

b) Telephone reference inquiries produce better results than mail. By telephone, a depth of detail can be acquired, and people given as references are usually more willing to speak frankly than to put the same comments in writing.

c) Reference information should be obtained *before* a full interview. Data can be checked, and selected areas for discussion or further probing can be chosen for the interview.

4. *Physical examination*.   The main purpose of the physical examination is to determine the type of work the applicant is physically best suited to perform. It shows one of several situations: (*a*) that the candidate is physically able to do certain types of work; (*b*) that he is fit for limited service only in specific jobs; (*c*) that with certain adjustments and treatments, he will be suited for jobs of a particular sort; or (*d*) that

he is physically unfit, and proper corrective action cannot be taken. Physical examinations help to raise the standard of physical fitness, to increase work output, to lower accident rates, to decrease turnover, and to lessen the amount of absenteeism caused by sickness.

5. *Tests.* This is the last personnel selection tool to be discussed. *Tests are measurements of personnel aspects secured by scientific methods of observing and recording in certain standard situations.* The measurements are normally qualitative and are believed to be related to success in performing the work. But tests determine what a candidate can do, not what he will do. A test score is an indication of the probability of the candidate's success or failure as determined by his possession of the attributes measured and the importance of these attributes in the work accomplishment.

There are on the market today a great number of tests designed to measure the many different attributes considered significant in personnel work. Among the many types of single-trait tests, the following are probably of greatest importance in office management: (1) the intelligence test, (2) the clerical test, (3) the personality test, and (4) the interest test. Figure 35 shows a comparison of these four types of tests, revealing for each one the contribution, general content, basic implication, names, and main purpose. The National Business Entrance Tests, sponsored jointly by the Administrative Management Society and the United Business Education Association, offer a battery of tests covering machine calculation, stenography, typing, bookkeeping, filing, and business fundamentals. Those who pass these tests are given a card or certificate of proficiency which is evidence of having successfully passed certain standardized clerical tests.

A 12-hour examination program is utilized for Certified Professional Secretary candidates. The examination, prepared annually, consists of personal adjustments and human relations, economics and business organization, business law, secretarial accounting, stenography, and secretarial procedures. Successful candidates are given a CPS identifying card and are permitted to wear a CPS pin.[1]

Several terms in connection with tests should be familiar to the office manager. These include:

a) Validity of test. This refers to the relationship between the test score and accepted or known facts about the attribute measured by the

---

[1] For further information on the National Entrance Tests, write the Administrative Management Society, Willow Grove, Pa.; for information on the Certified Professional Secretary tests, write National Secretaries Association, 222 West Eleventh Street, Kansas City, Mo.

Name	Contribution	General Content of Test	Basic Implications	Examples of Standard Tests	Main Purpose of Test
Intelligence and Mental Alertness Tests	Indicates one's adequacy in a number of types of work.	Problems on information and of judgment and reasoning. Questions dealing with contrast or comparison. Memory tasks.	What a person has absorbed is a fair indication of what he will or can absorb. Differences in background are not taken into consideration. Little indication of how the indicated ability may be applied.	Army Alpha (Original and Several Revisions) Benge Test of General Knowledge The Henmon-Nelson Test of Mental Ability The O'Rourke General Classification Test Otis Self-Administering Test of Mental Ability The Pressey Senior Classification and Verification Psychological Corporation Scot Company Mental Alertness Test	To make preliminary selection. To gain an insight to the applicant's ability to understand and to manage ideas.
Trade and Clerical Tests	Helps to show the degree of achievement possessed by a candidate for this specific type of work.	Questions appraising vocabulary level. Ability to notice details. Problems in simple calculations and arithmetic reasoning. Competency in performing clerical work.	Candidate having achievement of certain level and above will probably execute the job requirements most effectively.	Benge's Clerical Test Blackstone Stenographic Proficiency Tests Minnesota Vocational Test for Clerical Workers National Business Entrance Tests O'Rourke's Clerical Aptitude Test Psychological Corporation Shellow's Intelligence Test for Stenographers Thurstone Examination in Clerical Work, Form A	To determine applicant's knowledge of a specific trade or profession. To select candidates having at least a certain minimum of relative ability to perform work in a particular field.
Personality Tests	Indicates the presence or absence of a trait, or group of traits.	Single item questions which are answered with "Yes" or "No." Single words suggested— applicant names words which he associates with this single word.	Applicant will answer questions honestly. The makeup of the personality is related to the situational demands of a job.	Beckman Revision of Allport A-S Test California Test of Personality Heidbreder's Personal Traits Rating Scale, Form 2 Humm-Wadsworth Temperament Scale Laird's Personal Inventory C-2	To appraise those qualities which are pivotal in a situation and probably will determine the degree of future success of candidate on the job.
Interest Tests	Aims to determine the extent of the candidate's genuine interest in a particular type of work.	Questions to indicate the correct use or identity of machines and devices.	One's latent or developed interest in a certain type of work is closely related to the energy, persistence, and contribution which he gives to that work.	Brainard-Steward Specific Interest Inventory Strong's Vocational Interest Blank, Form A Thurstone Vocational Interest Schedule	To determine the degree of interest which a candidate has for different types of work.

FIG. 35. Comparison of various tests on significant factors.

test. To illustrate, the most desirable employees among the present employees should make a high score; the average employees, a lower score; and the least desirable employees, the lowest score.

b) Reliability of test. This deals with the consistency of the test in yielding similar results when given on different occasions. In other words, the same approximate results should always be obtained with the same group and the same test.

c) Standardization of test. When a test has been found, through a process of experimentation, to have both validity and reliability, it is commonly referred to as a standardized test.

d) Norms of test. A series of numbers indicating performance scores of large numbers of persons who have taken the test are called "norms." They serve as guides for comparison of scores.

Testing is a specialized field, and best results are usually obtained when the work is performed by qualified testing experts. Trained personnel, either on a part- or full-time basis, can be engaged.

CHAPTER TEN

USING THE OFFICE

MANUAL TO HELP

We have too many people who live without working,
and we have altogether too many who work without living.
—*Charles R. Brown*

To AN employee a manual can assist effectively in supplying not only organizational facts, but also in identifying the duties and responsibilities of occupants of specific jobs. Authorized and pertinent information dealing with the policies and practices of the enterprise; recommended systems, procedures, methods, and standards to be followed; and the regulations regarding employment can be given in a simple, direct, and uniform manner by means of manuals. *An office manual is a written record of information and instructions which concern and can be used to guide the employee's efforts in an enterprise.* Actually, it is a guidebook—a source for data believed essential for the highest performance of the job.

EVALUATION OF MANUALS

Essentially, an office manual is a device to assist in the orientation of employees. It can help to make instructions definite, to provide quick settlements of misunderstandings, to show each employee how his job fits into the total organization, and to point out how he can contribute to the achievements of office objectives as well as to maintain good relationships with other employees. On the other hand, manuals aid management members significantly. Manuals relieve management members of having to repeat similar information, explanations, or instructions. They not only force decisions on policies and procedures—thoughts about them must be put into writing—but they also provide constancy to them. Employees come and go, but the manual stays. The training of newcomers is enhanced. The delegation of authority is promoted by the use of manuals.[1] Furthermore, manuals assist in reducing gaps, obsolete activities, and needless office work duplication.

In contrast, there are some managers who do not advocate the use of manuals for any of a number of reasons. Among the more common criticisms are that manuals "cost too much," "are too much work," "stifle initiative," or "won't work in our case." In some cases, these objections are no doubt justifiable; but for many enterprises, the use of manuals appears to be beneficial. The great majority of nonusers of manuals are small companies where informal communication and mode of operations are considered sufficient.

---

1. Center authority and responsibility for the manual program.
2. Write to the level of the employee who will use the manual.
3. Maintain a distribution list—distribute only those manuals that are needed in each case.
4. Use color to emphasize identity of binder or printing matter.
5. Keep manual simple in arrangement of material and in language used.
6. Adopt adequate indexing and cross-referencing.
7. Use numerous visual aids—charts and illustrations.
8. Keep manuals up to date.
9. Highlight changes and revisions.
10. Audit the material periodically.

FIG. 36.   Basic requirements for success of office manuals.

Figure 36 lists the basic requirements for success of office manuals. More will be included about these requirements throughout the pages of this chapter.

TYPES OF OFFICE MANUALS

Different offices have need for different manuals. The type is determined by answering the question: "What is the purpose to be served?" In some instances, a single purpose only is served; while in others, several purposes are to be fulfilled. The number and the kind of purposes are determined by the individual circumstances.

Manuals can be written to cover a variety of subjects, including policies, organizational structure of the enterprise, employment, indoctrination, supervision, job instruction, standard work practices, computer

---

[1] Delegation of authority is discussed in Chapter 3, p. 39.

data processing, history of the enterprise, and specialized or departmental practices such as in the accounting, corresponding, filing, engineering, purchasing, or sales department. However, for convenience, the major types of manuals, along with their respective purposes, can be set forth as follows:

Type of Manual	*Purpose*
Manual of policies	To state the policies of the enterprise or office.
Manual of operations, or standard practices manual, or job instruction manual	To inform employees of established methods, procedures, and standards.
Manual of office rules and regulations, or handbook on employment	To give concise information on benefits, operating rules, and employment regulations.
Historical Manual	To provide historical information about the enterprise.
Multiple-purpose manual	To supply selected items from any area or subject deemed desirable and helpful in the work performance.

MANUAL OF POLICIES

A policy can be considered a basic guide to action. It prescribes the overall boundaries within which activities are to take place and hence reveals broad managerial intentions or forecasts broad courses of managerial action likely to take place under certain conditions. To illustrate, promoting employees solely on the basis of merit is a policy. It states the guide for promoting, but it does not tell who will be promoted. Likewise, the payment of salaries above the prevailing amounts in the community for similar work, consistent with the economic well-being of the enterprise, is another example of a policy. Knowing the policies of an enterprise provides the main framework around which all actions are based. Policies furnish the background for an understanding of why things are done as they are.

A manual of policies puts into writing the policies of an enterprise. It has been said that a policy does not really exist unless it is in writing. To decide each case on its individual merits and to convey this decision verbally is not in keeping with modern management thinking. Proponents of a manual of policies cite these advantages: (1) Written policies require managers to think through their courses of action and to predetermine what actions will be taken under various circumstances; (2) a general program of action for many matters is provided, and only the unusual or exceptional matter requires the attention of the top managers; (3) a framework is provided within which the manager can operate freely; and (4) written policies help to insure equitable treatment to all employees.

On the other hand, there are those who object to having a manual of policies. Among the important points they mention are the following: (1) Policies are extremely difficult to write accurately and completely—the interpretation of words and phrases sometimes leads to serious misunderstandings; (2) written policies make it difficult to keep policies flexible, as is frequently required by changing conditions; and (3) knowledge of policies should be confined to those persons charged with their execution—the top executive, department heads, or supervisors, as the case might be.

MANUAL OF OPERATIONS

A manual can serve as a convenient source for information on how the work is to be done. The authorized steps can be listed; and supplementary information, in the form of diagrams, sketches, and charts, can be included in order to clarify the data. The standards and guides to be followed are usually included.

The contents of this type of manual can be pointed toward any one or all of the following:

1. *Individual tasks and jobs.*   Illustrative is the manual which explains how to operate and use an adding machine. The importance of keeping accurate records can be emphasized and information included describing the parts and operations of an adding machine, practice lessons, and an explanation of the practices of the company. A glossary of terms is sometimes included to clarify the work.

2. *Departmental practices.*   Manuals of this type contain a statement of the duties of the department. Its divisions are defined, the supervisors listed, and their responsibilities indicated, along with outlines and procedures for operating. The work of departments, such as sales, purchasing, accounting, and research, is often set up and described in departmental manuals.

3. *General practices in a special field.*   This type of manual is becoming more popular, for it furnishes valuable general information which is usable in special lines of work. Its adoption is mainly in large offices, although in certain instances the small office can benefit from manuals of this type. Systems and procedures manuals and those for computer data processing are illustrative. Each of these vary considerably in makeup. However, a somewhat typical page from a systems and

procedures manual will give the number, title, and subtitle of the system or procedure, the organization units affected, a general statement of the system or procedure in one paragraph, an outline of the material classified by major headings, with important actions numbered and listed under each heading. Concluding are original issue date, revision date, and signature of authorizing manager.

MANUAL OF OFFICE RULES AND REGULATIONS

Manuals are an excellent medium in which to explain employee benefit plans, including such things as group insurance, hospitalization, and savings facilities. Questions regarding the use of the company library, cafeteria, and recreation club can also be answered. In addition, the prescribed guides for conduct are included and cover such items as sick allowances, the use of rest periods, conduct regarding smoking, solicitation for money in the office, the sale of tickets, hours of employment, holidays, vacations, office etiquette, rest periods, telephone usage, and recreational provisions. As already stated, a manual of this type is identified either as a manual of office rules and regulations or as a handbook on employment. However, for psychological reasons, the manual may be given a title like "You and the XYZ Company" or "Getting Along at XYZ." Such a manual helps to orientate and to inform the employee by giving him specific answers to all the elements of his work surroundings, thus promoting understanding and harmonious relationships. Figure 37 shows a sample of the type of information included in this kind of manual.

HISTORICAL MANUAL

Many employers feel that it is important to give employees information regarding the history of the company—its beginning, growth, accomplishments, present management, and current status. This gives the employee an insight into the tradition and thinking behind the enterprise with which he is associated. It probably makes for better understanding, increases morale, and helps the employee to feel that he "belongs"—that he is a part of the company. Giving an employee a picture of the whole helps him to fit himself into the total picture. Manuals, of course, are excellent means for conveying this type of information to employees. The story of the enterprise usually can be told on several pages; and quite frequently, it can be a part of a message written by a major officer. Historical information is commonly included as the introductory portion to a manual of office rules and regulations.

GENERAL OFFICE ROUTINES

DESKS—Keep your desk clean. It's a workbench, not a catchall. Never allow a lot of old-fashioned relics to accumulate on it. File everything away in its natural place, and dispose of obsolete matter. (The job of filing is an important one and is not to be neglected or allowed to pile up.)

Avoid having decorations on the desk that might tip and spill, such as flower containers, ink bottles, sponge cups, etc. Keep such things in safer places.

Clear all desks and tables before leaving the building. Any papers or letters of a confidential nature must be put away, never left on the desk top. All lights are to be turned off, fans and ventilators disconnected, and blinds raised. Typewriters should be covered when not being used.

DUSTING—Each office is to be thoroughly dusted each morning—during the day too if necessary. No one need resent dusting—it's part of the job.

Pens should be filled, pencils sharpened and water bottles filled first thing in the morning. See to it that ash trays are kept clean throughout the day. If blotters are used, make sure soiled ones are replaced.

Typewriters should be dusted morning and night, type cleaner applied weekly.

SUPPLIES—If you are responsible for handling supplies for the office, check them regularly and make sure that you are not running low. Keep a list at your desk of supplies that will soon need to be requisitioned (use form 527 for ordering). All requisitions must be authorized by the department head.

HOURS—Arrange hours if possible so the office will not be unattended at any time. If it is impossible for someone to be present during lunch hour, do not leave without making arrangements with someone else to take any important calls.

CALLERS—It is much better to have an understanding with your superior regarding his wishes in the matter of announcing callers, the persons he wishes to see and those he does not, rather than to guess at the proper procedure in each instance.

Keep an accurate, up to date list or notebook of telephone numbers and addresses, business as well as personal. Such a list should be readily accessible. Add to it regularly so it will be of value both to you and your superior.

Source: Butler Brothers, "Secretaries' and Stenographers' Handbook" (Chicago, 1946), p. 20.
Reproduced here by special permission.

FIG. 37.   Page of a manual used by a large national distributor of general merchandise.

MULTIPLE-PURPOSE MANUAL

This type of manual represents a combination of any two or all of the types discussed above. The company's needs, the size of the enterprise, and the philosophy of the top managers usually determine the makeup. The outline of a multiple-purpose manual might include the following:

1. Title.
2. Foreword.
3. Table of Contents.

4. Company History.
5. General Policies of Company.
6. Organization.
7. Company Departments—Functions, Authorities, and Responsibilities.
8. Office Regulations.
9. Office Supplies and Maintenance.
10. Personnel Points—Hiring, Promoting, Terminating, Sick Leave, Employee Benefits, and Social Activities.
11. Miscellaneous.
12. Index.

SOURCES FOR MANUAL MATERIAL

Probably one of the best sources of material for a manual is manuals used by other enterprises. Looking over what has been included in manuals of another company suggests what topics might be covered. However, the manual should be personalized to meet the particular needs of an enterprise.

Additional data can be secured from a number of other sources. Such data might include (1) minutes of board of directors' meetings, (2) reports of executive conferences, (3) speeches and published articles of executives, (4) bulletins and company circulars, (5) agreements with employees and contracts with unions, (6) grievance records, (7) company magazines or similar publications, and (8) interviews with executives, especially the personnel manager, training director, and supervisors.

Experience shows that, with time, it will be desirable to eliminate certain material and to add other material. The additional material might be secured from the above sources or, because of the unique nature of the information, may be secured from a special source. For example, instructions in the correct use of a new office machine would probably be secured from the manufacturer or seller.

PREPARATION OF MANUALS

Some orderly process must be followed in the preparation of manuals if they are to be inclusive and to be completed within a reasonable period of time. The process followed depends a great deal upon the individual in charge of this work. In general, however, it will be helpful to follow a procedure along these lines:

1. *Announce to all members of the enterprise that a manual is to be prepared.* Solicit their suggestions and ideas as to what should be

included. Appointing a committee of employees often encourages their participation in the preparation of the manual. As a result, better understanding and greater acceptance and use are usually gained. Special attention should be directed to supervisors, for they are usually rich sources of excellent material.

2. *Draw up a list of all the subjects to be covered by the manual.* The purpose of the manual, the cost, and managerial judgment will determine, for the most part, what items are included. Proper subheadings should be made under each main topic, and the list should be arranged according to the contemplated main divisions or sections of the manual. A big time-saver in this respect is to use a separate card for each topic and file behind guides. By this means, material can be classified quickly and the list or outline changed with a minimum of effort.

A logical arrangement of the material is most commonly used, but this sequence is not necessarily the most effective in all cases. Consideration should be given to placing the vital information or that which is most interesting in the beginning, using the last portion of the list for data of less importance.

3. *Write the information under each subject.* It is advisable to use headings—major and minor—so that the material is well organized and the reader can follow it easily. Check the source data to help insure accuracy in all writing. Source material can be numbered and indexed, and this means of identification tied in with the writing by means of marginal notes. Keep the prospective reader in mind—write so he will want to read the manual and understand what it is intended to mean. A simple, friendly, and sincere style is best. Short words and sentences should be employed. Narrative style is common, but the playscript format (similar to that used for a drama or play) is very effective. Include charts, cartoons, diagrams, and examples of proper forms, letters, and reports in order to gain greater clarity. These illustrations should be in an inexpensive, rough form until it is decided, as described below, whether they will be included in the final manual. All material should be presented in the "normal flow of work" sequence. The amount of detail depends upon the importance of the subject.

4. *Prepare a limited number of copies for key executives, supervisors, employee or union representatives, and several key employees.* Have them read the manual and submit criticisms and suggestions. Quite often, better ways of expression are found in this way. Sometimes, subjects can be combined, major items previously overlooked can be added, minor points strengthened, and the entire manual improved.

5. *Revise the manual and give it to top management members for approval.* Corrections and suggestions from the previous step are

incorporated. It is well to include a separate statement to the effect that the entire contents are in agreement with the philosophy of top management members and are acceptable to the employees.

6. *Send the approved manuscript to the printer or the party doing the actual mechanical production work.* The manual can be published by any of several different methods, including xerography, mimeograph, offset printing, or letterpress. The quantity, appearance, and cost will probably determine the process used. Details regarding size, paper, and type of binding must also be decided. Generally, it is well to seek competent advice in these matters.

The size 6¼ x 4½ inches is excellent for a booklet intended for carrying in the pocket. If the manual is to be used as a reference book on a desk, an 11 x 8½-inch size is very satisfactory. Other popular sizes include 9⅛ x 6 inches, 8½ x 5½ inches, and 5⅛ x 3¾ inches. Pages of these sizes can be cut, with minimum waste, from sheet sizes usually carried by the printer.[2]

The number and size of the pages in the booklet generally determine the weight of paper used. When the number of pages does not exceed about 24, a thick paper can be used; but where a greater number of pages is involved, a thinner stock is used, to eliminate unnecessary bulk. For page sizes under about 8½ x 5½ inches, a paper of about 60 pounds is used. When the size is greater, paper of about 70 pounds is employed.

Make the headings stand out on the page by the use of white space around them, or color may be employed. Color increases the cost; but in many cases, the effect brought about by such things as a colored border, headline, or illustration justifies the additional expense. For additional suggestions see Figure 38.

The type of binding may be either side or saddle wire stitching, screw post, prong fasteners, ring binder, and wire or plastic edge binding. The choice will depend primarily upon usage, amount of material, appearance, and cost.

DISTRIBUTION OF MANUALS

It is paramount in the distribution of the manuals to provide a copy to everyone concerned with and in need of the information the manual

---

[2] In the case of loose-leaf and many bound manuals, it is customary to give the dimension of the binding side first. Thus, an 11 x 8-inch size means the binding is on an 11-inch side. The dimensions used in this discussion follow this practice. In contrast, and at times somewhat confusingly, in specifying dimensions of index cards, the horizontal dimension is named first, followed by the vertical dimension. For example, an 8 x 5 card means 8 inches horizontally and 5 inches vertically.

PAGE SIZE—

If printed, the 6 x 9-inch page size is effective. This is the typical book size.
If typed, the 8½ x 11-inch page size will be preferred by most employees.

ARRANGEMENT OF MATERIAL—

Place sections most frequently used at front of manual.
Related sections should be placed close together and interrelated by cross-references.
Set sections apart by stiff divider page of different-colored paper.
Either tab sections for ready reference, or use a divider of page size to facilitate a margin index.

REMEMBER TO—

Make the cover attractive by using a clear, brief title and well-selected artwork.
Include a table of contents and an index so that the reader can quickly find what he is looking for.

FIG. 38.   Helpful suggestions for preparation of manuals.

contains. The extent of distribution depends upon the size of the enterprise; in most cases, one copy of the manual should be available for ready reference in at least each department or division. In cases where manuals pertain to specific jobs, copies should be readily available to every employee on such jobs.

To increase the readership of the manual, it is sometimes given to the employee only during an interview. His attention is directed to specific pages, and he is encouraged to read the entire booklet. In some cases, depending upon the type of manual, it is mailed to the employee's home with an accompanying letter. Forewarning that the manual is to be used as the subject for a forthcoming meeting or group discussion is a very effective means of encouraging readership. In addition, sometimes the employee is requested to sign and to return an enclosed card in the manual as evidence of reading the complete booklet; and in other instances, questions are asked on the card to measure the employee's understanding of the manual contents.

MANUAL MAINTENANCE

The problem of keeping the manual up to date is ever present. In most enterprises, changes are taking place constantly, owing to new work being added or improvements in current work being made. Revisions of and additions to manuals are constantly in process. New pages must replace the old and be distributed to all holders of the manuals. These changes may be covered either by single sheets or by entire supplements. Frequently, amendments are written on colored paper to attract attention to the change. Also, notations made in red ink in the manual will point out those parts which have been changed, omitted, or amended. When many changes cause the manual to be difficult to read and use, it should be rewritten.

All changes in manuals should be cleared through a central control unit so that proper authorization and conformity in results are obtained. If this is not done, needless confusion and misunderstanding will result. The revised sheets should follow the established form of the manual. New material will probably be added every three to six months, together with certain modifications in the old material. Limited research shows that nearly 90 percent of all managers prefer a three-ring binder, which facilitates the insertion of revised sheets.

THE THREE R'S OF MANUALS

An old saying is that the three R's of manuals are reading, reference, and revision. Adequate attention should be given these R's for in large measure, they regulate the real contribution of a manual and govern whether it is used and does the job intended for it. The manual writers, committees, or managers can judge a manual against these three considerations, but it is also helpful to ask rank and file users what they think of the manual using these three R's as a guide. Either personal interviews or questionnaires can be used. Under reading, inquiries should be directed to reveal whether the manual is easy to read. Is the type size proper, are margins adequate? Are the paragraphs about the right length, and is the writing style fluent and does it assist in conveying the meaning of the material? Further, are illustrations used freely in order to expedite understanding? Under the second R, or reference, are included considerations such as providing clear instructions for the manual's use and a logical numbering arrangement for sections. All titles and headings should be truly indicative of the respective material presented. Finally, under the third R, or revision, every part of the manual must be completely up to date. The addition of inserts giving changes should pose no problem and the locating of such changes by the user should be expedited.